COMBAT AIRCRAFT SERIES

AH-64 Apache

BILL GUNSTON

OSPREY PUBLISHING LONDON

Printed in
Belgium

Published in 1986 by
Osprey Publishing Ltd
Member Company of the George Philip Group
12–14 Long Acre, London WC2E 9LP

This book is copyrighted under the Berne Convention. All rights reserved. Apart from any fair dealing for the purpose of private study, research, criticism or review, as permitted under the Copyright Act, 1956, no part of this publication may be reproduced, stored in a retrieval system, or transmitted in any form or by any means, electronic, electrical, chemical, mechanical, optical, photocopying, recording or otherwise, without the prior permission of copyright owner. Enquiries should be addressed to the Publishers.

© Copyright 1986 Bedford Editions Ltd.

British Library Cataloguing in Publication Data

Gunston, Bill
AH-64 Apache.—(Osprey combat aircraft)
1. Apache (Helicopter)—History
I. Title
629.133'352 UG1233

ISBN 0-85045-721-1

Typeset by Flair plan Photo-typesetting Ltd.
Printed by Proost International Book Production, Turnhout, Belgium.

Colour artworks by Seb Quigley, © Bedford Editions Ltd.
Cutaway drawing: © Pilot Press Ltd.
Diagrams: TIGA and Mike Keep.
Photographs: The publishers would like to thank McDonnell Douglas (Hughes) and the US Department of Defense for the photographs reproduced in this book.

The Author

BILL GUNSTON, former RAF pilot and flying instructor, is an internationally acknowledged expert on aircraft and aviation affairs. He is the author of numerous books on the subject, is a frequent broadcaster, was technical editor of "Flight International" and technology editor of "Science Journal", and is assistant compiler of "Jane's All The World's Aircraft". He is the author of another book in this series, *MiG-23/-27 Flogger.*

Contents

Chapter 1:
Design and Development 3
Chapter 2:
Technical Features 9
Chapter 3:
Apache Sensors 17
Chapter 4:
Apache Weapons 33
Chapter 5 :
Joining the Army 41
Chapter 6:
Marine and Navy Apaches 46
Specifications 48

1

Design and Development

FEW FLYING machines are as menacing as the armed helicopter, and no armed helicopter is more menacing than the aptly named Apache. Though dull olive grey in colour, the Apaches look black as they come thundering in, making the air for miles around vibrate with the mighty power of their threshing blades. Like awesome armoured insects, they close with the enemy, shrugging off the hail of fire directed against them and finally picking off thick-skinned tanks as if they were flies. Within seconds the throbbing attackers have vanished, leaving behind a scene of carnage and desolation.

Undeniably, the Apache is impressive, and calculated to strike fear into its enemies. All the senior commanders of the US Army from President Reagan down have singled it out for special praise. Not untypical was the comment of Brig-Gen Ellis D.Parker, Deputy Director for Requirements: "It gives corps and division commanders the opportunity to capitalize on more of the principles of war than with any other system they have." But all this is only one side of the coin.

The other side is that, whereas the Apache was planned to cost $1.4 million, each of today's helicopters sets back the US taxpayer almost ten times that amount. And Warsaw Pact armies are more completely defended against air attack than any others in history, with vast numbers of highly mobile SAMs capable with one shot of blowing an Apache into small fragments. Controversy over the viability of battlefield helicopters will continue, but the point must be noted that no nation makes greater use of them than the Soviet Union. Moreover, in the new Havoc, believed to be the Mi-28, that country has paid the Apache the most sincere form of compliment possible, in the form of an apparently direct copy.

Early helicopters were incapable of carrying many weapons, and it was not until the 1960s that purpose-designed armed helicopters were considered. The first to be built was small, a development of the Bell 47 Sioux called the Model 207 Sioux Scout. With only 260hp, it did well to carry a crew of two—for the first time in a slim tandem cockpit reminiscent of a fighter—and a chin turret with two machine guns. Indeed, small wings were fitted to help unload the rotor and provide attachments for rockets or other weapons. Significantly, the gunner was in the nose and the pilot behind and slightly higher.

High-performance requirement

With increasing involvement in Vietnam, and belated recognition that existing armed helicopters were merely ordinary transport helicopters on to which a few weapons had been fastened, the US Army spent 1964-65 devising a specification for a specially designed armed helicopter. Rejoicing in the title of Advanced Aerial Fire Support System (AAFSS), the requirement called for a machine of unprecedented performance and capability, with the ability to fly and fight extremely close to the ground even at night or in bad weather. In March 1966 Lockheed was picked over 11 other contestants for what promised to be a giant programme.

The first of ten prototypes of the AH-56A Cheyenne began its flight test programme on 21 September 1967. Powered by a 3,925shp General Electric T64 engine, it was in some ways almost an autogyro or even an aeroplane, because in cruising flight much of the lift was provided by a wing. The main rotor was almost feathered, and "almost the entire engine output" was supplied to the tail gearbox where there was not only the usual anti-torque rotor but also a propeller giving forward thrust. Cruising speed was 242mph (389km/h). Avionics were said to be "more complicated than a B-52", with inertial and doppler navigation, terrain-following radar and amazingly complex systems for aiming a nose turret with a Minigun or grenade launcher and a belly turret with a 30mm cannon. Missiles and rockets were fired from under the wings. So great were the problems and costs that this bold and impressive machine never went into production.

The Army's urgent needs in Vietnam were met by the simpler AH-1 HueyCobra, produced very quickly by Bell as a private venture. In a brilliantly successful programme, the Cobra has been continuously upgraded and developed to such an extent that today's AH-1W for the Marine Corps has an installed horsepower of 3,392, compared with the original AH-1's 1,000! To a rough approximation, lifting ability is proportional to installed power, but the Cobras find it difficult to operate except by day and in clear visibility.

Warsaw Pact tank threat

Accordingly, in 1972 the US Army at last got its act together and, picking up where the AAFSS had left off, launched a programme for an Advanced Attack Helicopter (AAH). It was virtually forced into doing so by the awesome and increasing power of the Warsaw Pact armoured forces facing Western Europe. It was recognised that the capabilities promised by the cancelled Cheyenne were not merely desirable but absolutely essential.

Above: 1973 mock-up of the Hughes YAH-64 Apache, forerunner of the winning design, which was to change considerably.

Four years into the AAH programme, in 1976, the Hon Edward A. Miller, Assistant Secretary of the Army (R&D), said: "The AAH's night vision and adverse weather capability, in concert with its agility, speed and vertical acceleration, will deprive any advancing armored force of its security. The AAH's

Below: The two prototypes of Bell's rival YAH-63 losing design which, among other things, put the pilot in front of the gunner and also featured a tricycle-type landing gear.

Above: Two Lockheed AH-56A Cheyennes flying over the test facility at Oxnard, California, 1968. The AH-56A was cancelled.

maneuverability will enable it to destroy tanks in rocky or heavily wooded areas where previously they would have been relatively safe from air attack.

"Soviet and Warsaw Pact units are well equipped for air defense, and the AAH is designed to survive in the hostile environment these anti-aircraft weapons will create. Its ability will make it a very elusive target, and it is capable of sustaining (*sic*, he meant to say 'surviving') hits from 12.7mm machine-gun rounds and, in some vital areas, 23mm weapons. It is also equipped with an effective infra-red suppression system to protect it from heat-seeking missiles. The AAH, with its night and adverse-weather capabilities, will greatly reduce the qualitative armor advantage now enjoyed by the East."

Five-company competition

The AAH promised to be a major programme, and five companies fought to win it: Bell Helicopter, Boeing Vertol, Hughes Helicopters, Lockheed and Sikorsky. The one firm that could not lose was General Electric, whose specially designed T700 turboshaft engine had already been picked not only for the AAH but also for the even more numerous UTTAS (Utility Tactical Transport Aircraft System) which was won by the Sikorsky S-70 (UH-60A) Black Hawk. As both helicopters were required to be twin-engined, GE was fairly safe in planning to build 5,000 of their new engine. But for the AAH itself it was a different story. Bids were all in by 1 March 1973, and on 22 June of that year the Army picked Bell and Hughes to receive competitive development contracts. Each was to build two flight prototypes and one GTV (ground test vehicle). In addition, Hughes received an award to develop a special gun for the AAH, Bell electing to use the XM188 gun by General Electric. This partly explained the startling difference in the two development contracts, Bell's being for $44.7 million and Hughes' being priced at $70.3 million.

Bell's design was the Model 409, given the official designation YAH-63. It was the smallest helicopter Bell could design while still meeting the severe mission requirements. The T700 engines were placed quite low down behind the rotor gearbox, the cowls being blended into the fuselage. Ahead of the rotor the entire forward fuselage was occupied by the tandem cockpits, the pilot being in the nose and the CPG (copilot/gunner) behind and slightly above. The XM188 gun, a three-barrel 30mm weapon related to the M61 fighter gun, was mounted under the extreme nose, the visionics and sight system being further back underneath. Landing gear was of the fixed tricycle type, with twin steerable nosewheels. The slender tailboom was inclined upwards to give clearance for the sweptback underfin at the tail, which was almost as big as the upper fin carrying the small horizontal tail on top, the tail rotor being on the end of the tailboom. The main rotor had just two large blades, the diameter being 51ft 10in (15.54m).

Bearing in mind that the missions and the engines

were the same, the Hughes Model 77, designated YAH-64, could hardly have been more different in design. The engines were placed in separate boxes standing away from the rather lumpy humpbacked fuselage, driving via diagonal shafts from separate gearboxes looking like small jet inlets on the front of each engine. The transparencies over the cockpits were huge, and the crew were seated the other way round compared with the Bell; the CPG being markedly lower down and in front.

Likewise, the positions of the sight system and gun were reversed, the sight being in the nose and the gun underneath. Landing gear was of the tailwheel type, the main units having ungainly long legs sloping diagonally backward and supported by shock struts attached between their mid-points and the longeron at the base of the canopies.

Prototype tail details

The tail comprised a very low-mounted tailplane (horizontal stabilizer) and a slightly swept fin carrying the tail rotor half-way up. This rotor was unusual in that, to reduce noise, the four blades were not spaced at 90°. The main rotor also had four blades, and was remarkably small, though, like the Bell rotor, it was fully articulated with pitch-change bearings, flapping hinges and drag hinges.

The Hughes GTV, called AV01, ran its rotors for the first time exactly two years after the contract award, on 22 June 1975, and by 19 September it had completed the 50 hours of running necessary before first flight of either flying prototype. The latter was designated AV02 and AV03, meaning Air Vehicle 02 and 03; AV02 made its first flight at the Hughes flight centre at Palomar, California, on 30 September 1975, one day inside the deadline. The first Bell YAH-63 flew next day, right on the deadline, at Arlington, Texas. Hughes' AV03 flew on 22 November 1975, while the second Bell flew on 21 December.

By this time the Hughes design had gone through a metamorphosis. Most striking of the changes were at the tail, where the attachments for the tailplane at the bottom of the tailboom remained unused. Instead the fin was extended upwards, with a strange kinked shape and a cambered (sideways lifting) aerofoil profile, and the tailplane was placed right at the top, projecting far ahead of the top of the fin. The nose was redesigned with different sensors, large compartments were added on each side of the nose for avionics, and the cockpit and canopy were totally redesigned with giant flat transparent panes in strong frames, the right-hand windows serving as the access doors. Finally, in these initial modifications, the main-rotor mast was extended upwards by 9.5in (240mm), because in extreme flight manoeuvres the

Below: The Hughes Air Vehicles AV02 and 03 on test in 1976. Though clearly Apaches, they differed in almost every respect from today's helicopter, notably in the nose and tail.

blades could rub across the top of the canopy.

During Phase I testing availability of the two AVs had been consistently above 86 per cent, considered an exceptional achievement. A total of 850 hours had been flown without accident, at speeds up to 225mph (362km/h) forwards and 52mph (83.7km/h) to the side and rear, at weights 4,000lb (1,814kg) higher than the design mission weight and with lateral and vertical accelerations never before reached by a helicopter. A sustained rate of climb of 3,500ft/min (17.8m/s) had been demonstrated, and prolonged tests with the company's own XM230 Chain Gun and 2.75in rockets had shown the YAH-64 to be a very stable firing platform.

Missile armament

In the AAH specification the primary armament was to be eight TOW anti-tank missiles in two quadruple launchers, though the prototypes demonstrated their ability to carry double this number. TOW requires a human operator to guide it along the line of sight all the way to the target, and this obviously tends to force the helicopter to expose itself throughout this time to enemy fire. In 1973 the US Army began development of a new-generation anti-tank missile which would not need this form of guidance. As explained later, this emerged as AGM-114 Hellfire, and in a major specification change in February 1976 this missile replaced TOW as the primary weapon.

Bell and Hughes worked furiously to bring their prototypes to the stage at which, in mid-June 1976, they could be delivered to Edwards AFB, California, for Army competitive evaluation. At the last minute one YAH-63 had an accident, on 4 June, and the Bell GTV had to be frantically brought up to flight status as the replacement.

This did not help Bell's chances, and another factor in Hughes' favour was the company's decision at the start of the programme that it would need a big industrial team to ensure that the highest possible level of specialist expertise would be applied to every major part. Apart from GE for the engines, this team comprised: Bendix, electric power system, and main transmission shafts and couplings; Bertea, hydraulic flight controls; Garrett, engine IR suppressed exhausts and integrated pressurized air systems; Hi-Shear, canopy and crew escape system; Litton (Precision Gear Division), engine-nose and main transmission gearboxes; Menasco, landing gears; Solar, gas-turbine APU (auxiliary power unit); Sperry, autostabilization; Teledyne Ryan, airframe structure; Teledyne Systems, fire-control computer; Tool Research and Engineering, main and tail rotor blades; and Western Gear, intermediate and tail rotor gearboxes.

At the end of 1976 it all came right for the Hughes team. The AH-64 was announced the winner, and

Below: Firing some of the first FFARs (folding-fin aircraft rockets) from AV02, in effect the very first Apache prototype. At this time no operational sensors were carried.

the company also won the gun competition with its unique Chain Gun. Hughes immediately received a $317.7 million contract for FSD (full-scale development) of the proposed production helicopter, including the construction of three more prototypes—AV04, 05 and 06—the last two with airframes subcontracted to Teledyne Ryan at San Diego.

Throughout 1977 Hughes flew the two prototypes at Palomar, testing and evaluating a "Mod 1" package of changes which earlier flying had shown to be desirable. These changes included a further 6in (152mm) increase in main rotor mast height, swept-back tips to the main-rotor blades to reduce compressibility, a redesign of the tailplane to have a reversed planform (straight leading edge and tapered trailing edge), a 3in (76mm) increase in diameter of the tail rotor, and installation of the first pattern of IR suppressed exhaust using not the engine-driven fans originally specified but the Hughes Black Hole type of passive cooling box using self-induced airflow to mix with the hot gas.

Phase II testing

These changes had all been flown by May 1978. By this time AV02 and 03, after a combined total of 720 hours, were grounded in order to be brought up to full production standard for Phase II testing. This 56-month programme, costed at $390 million including the three extra prototypes, was the final long haul that had to be completed prior to the start of production. Modifications kept being introduced. When prototypes 02 and 03 resumed flying, respectively in November and December 1978, they incorporated the Mod 2 package which included all wiring for the mission avionics (though the vital sensors had still not been selected). Completely new avionics bays were constructed, starting near the nose and extending back under the wing, enclosing the upper part of each main gear on the way.

Even more obvious was continuing uncertainty over the horizontal tail. The fixed T-tail was satisfactory in most conditions, but at extremely low level—so-called NOE (nap of the Earth) flying—it let the tail sink down and the nose point skywards, demanding major forward stick movements at times when cockpit workload was high in any case. AV03 flew with a low tailplane, but something close to the definitive tail was not seen until the first of the new pre-production prototypes, AV04, flew on 31 October 1979.

Here was yet another new arrangement, with an all-moving "stabilator" mounted low down right at the back of the helicopter extending from just above the very tip of the tailboom. This enlarged surface was driven by a hydraulic power unit linked into the flight-control and autostab system to tilt the machine when necessary but in normal flight to preserve a horizontal attitude no matter what the circumstances. The new tail also had a vertical fin 3in (76mm) taller carrying a modified tail rotor a full 30in (0.76m) higher up. Even this was not quite the answer, and on 14 March 1980 AV04 flew with a smaller stabilator, followed two days later by the first flight of the AV06 which also introduced a tail rotor of 10in (254mm) greater diameter.

Back in March 1979 AV02 had carried out the first (ground) firing of a Hellfire missile, followed later by airborne shots against designated targets. In October 1979 02 carried out the first autonomous firing, designating the target itself with its own Martin Marietta TADS. But its sister, ship 03, was fitted with rival sensors by Northrop Nortronics, and it was not until March 1980 that the Martin installation was announced as the winner. This naturally affected not only the shape of the nose but also the giant side avionics panniers. Yet another visible change was that the flat glass cockpit panels were replaced by single-curvature bulged windows giving a view almost directly downwards or to the rear, though downwards view is slightly limited by the long avionics bays.

The only major setback in the programme came in November 1980 when 04 was destroyed in a mid-air collision in no way due to any fault in the helicopter. This machine had just completed a programme of weapon trials using all planned types of armament, and 02 and 06 continued the work using the Pilot's Night Vision System (PNVS) in an important series of night firings.

President Reagan signed the FY82 (Fiscal Year 1982) Defense Bill on 19 December 1981 in which was an item for $537.5 million for the first 11 production Apaches. Hughes announced plans to build an assembly plant on a virgin site at Mesa, Arizona, and this opened in February 1983. On 30 September 1983 PV01, the first production vehicle, was rolled out.

2
Technical Features

THE HEART of any helicopter is its rotor system, and that of the Apache is a carefully considered blend of traditional practice and new technology. Though it has passed through important stages of modification, the main rotor has always been fully articulated and had four blades of relatively small diameter resulting in unusually high disc loading (as in the small Hughes Cayuse/Defender family). Each of the four interchangeable blades has a broad chord and a highly cambered aerofoil section. As noted previously, the tips are raked backwards to reduce compressibility problems on the advancing blades. For transport by cargo aircraft each blade can readily be folded through 90° or removed and stowed.

Rotor blade structure

Each blade has five parallel spars of high-strength stainless steel, separated and lined by structural tubes of glassfibre. Laminated skins of thin stainless steel are wrapped round from the front, the number of laminations very rapidly increasing at the root to form a solid stack of retention straps through-bolted together. The trailing portion of each blade is of composite honeycomb structure bonded on separately. TRE Advanced Structures Division were required to demonstrate sustained operation under the most severe conditions with one steel skin cracked across and any one spar shot through.

At the root the multiple laminates are allowed to pivot upwards by an offset flapping hinge, and to rock to front and rear in the plane of the disc by elastomeric lead/lag dampers. Anti-vibration masses are attached at front and rear of each root on the lead/lag tie rods. Pitch changes are introduced in the usual way by vertical tie rods from the upper (rotating) swashplate, the non-rotating lower swashplate being tilted according to flight-control input demands by three powerful Parker Bertea hydraulic actuators between the pilot's seat and the main gearbox. Following major hydraulic failure the system automatically switches to Sperry secondary back-up FBW (fly-by-wire) electrical signalling.

An unusual feature is that all major stresses are transmitted via a fixed rotor mast from the bottom of which the helicopter is hung via four tubular vee-struts. The main gearbox is hung under the centre of the fixed mast and drives via a tubular shaft passing up the centre to the rotor hub spinning on roller bearings at the top of the fixed mast. This provides dual redundant load paths, and allows the transmission to be removed while keeping the rotor in place. No bearing lubrication is needed in the main rotor, and the intermediate and tail-rotor gearboxes are

Below: Thanks to its sheer power the Apache is agile. Putting on full power and slamming the cyclic stick forward for maximum forwards acceleration puts the Apache into this attitude.

packed with grease. Critical parts of the transmission are protected by ESR (electro-slag remelted) steel of very high strength. The whole dynamic system is thus ballistically tolerant, and has flown for over one hour after loss of all lubricating oil.

The tail rotor is especially very powerful. Its great thrust surprises the pupil pilot, because any attempt to turn on the ground can roll the Apache sideways on its soft and stalky legs, and it is easy to slide the tail sideways even on dry concrete. This rotor has its two pairs of high-lift blades set at the optimum angle for noise attentuation, which is about 55°/125°. Like the main-rotor blades the tail rotor has leading-edge deicer strips of the electro-thermal type, the supplier being Sierracin, which also provides the canopies and transparent blast shield between the cockpits.

In May 1983 Hughes completed wind-tunnel testing of a dramatically different new tail rotor operating on the so-called Flexbeam principle. The new tail rotor has a diameter of 112in (2.845m), compared with 110in for the normal rotor. Each consists of two pairs of blades mounted at 90° to each other, but the structure is wholly novel. All major loads are carried by a Flexbeam, an elastically tailored glassfibre spar which extends from tip to tip along the centre of each blade-pair. Over the outer ends of the beam are attached the blade airfoils, connected at their inboard ends to hollow pitchcases surrounding the inner part of each half of the beam. Laminated elastomeric snubbers always tend to centre the pitchcases relative to the beam, and elastomeric damping pads mount the flexbeam to the hub. The new rotor is not only lighter and cheaper but has no bearings, needs no maintenance and appears to have infinite fatigue life. It may become standard in 1987, and be retrofitted on Apaches already built.

Airframe construction

Teledyne Ryan Aeronautical, of San Diego, builds the complete airframe, comprising the fuselage, wings, tailboom, horizontal tail (called the stabilator) and the tail-rotor pylon (which most people would call the fin). The wings are easily disconnected at the roots of the two main spars, for air transport or storage, and they incorporate hardpoints for two

Below: Standing on the roof aft of the cockpit, a maintenance engineer has access all round the main rotor hub. Many parts are designed to withstand hits by 23mm cannon shells.

Below: Army specialists received their initial training at the McDonnell Douglas Mesa plant. Here an NCO service engineer inspects the curious tail rotor, with blades crossing at 55°.

Above: Probably destined soon to be instructing others, these were among the first troops to specialize in the complicated avionics. These line-replaceable units are in the right-hand bay.

pylons each, as well as a trailing-edge flap which was originally intended for use in manouevres but was not adopted and is now normally locked. The simple stabilator is pivoted near its leading edge to the top of the tail end of the tailboom, aft of the fin. Its widely variable angle of incidence is controlled via Hamilton Standard electronics by Simmonds hydraulic actuators, and as an emergency backup the Sperry fly-by-wire system can provide sufficient control power for a safe recovery to base.

The tail pylon is bolted to the top of the tailboom and carries the tail rotor near the top on the left side. The transmission, housed in a spine fairing along the top of the tailboom, is made of special materials such as ESR, a very little titanium, and 7049 aluminium alloy. Thick collars protect vital areas against gunfire, all elements being designed to operate for one hour after receiving ballistic (projectile) damage or total loss of oil. The right-angle final drive gearbox to the tail rotor is cooled by a special AiResearch fan, with the ram inlet in the front of the gearbox fairing.

The Menasco main landing gears could hardly be simpler. Each wheel, with hydraulic brake, is carried on the end of a plain tube pivoted to the bottom of the fuselage so that it is free to swing backwards and upwards. It is prevented from doing so by a shock strut pivoted half-way down the leg and to a large trunnion at the top of the fuselage under the edge of the canopy. This shock strut resists normal landings at gross weight at a vertical speed of 10ft/s, and emergency descents at 42ft/s with virtually certain crew survival. For air transport the strut can be depressurized to let the aircraft sink almost to the ground to reduce overall height. The tailwheel is attached to a yoke pivoted to the tail end of the tailboom, being free to castor except when locked by the pilot in the fore/aft direction.

Survivability features

At the start of the design of the original Model 77 it was obvious that some form of redundancy had to be provided not only in the structure of the airframe but also in the operative systems. Most of the structure is conventional, but with generous thicknesses of material and duplicated load paths to ensure survival even after severe local battle damage. Hughes was not required to demonstrate actual sustained flight following the severance of crucial parts of the helicopter, but the company believes the Apache to have a degree of airframe damage tolerance not even approached by any other helicopter. A diagram shows some of the fundamental design features which are hoped to ensure crew survivability even after a crash impact at a vertical velocity of 42ft (12.8m)/s. Impact energy is absorbed by the long-travel landing gears and by crushing of the lower-fuselage structure. The gun would be forced straight up into the space between the cockpits, while the seats can collapse vertically downwards in a controlled manner to minimise accelerations imparted to the occupants.

Flight control system

In the case of the systems, most services are duplicated, with routings widely separated wherever possible. Perhaps the most crucial system of all is the flight controls, and here the obvious answer at first seemed to be a dually redundant back-up mechanical system. Boldly, the decision was taken to design instead a

HUGHES AH-64 APACHE CUTAWAY DRAWING KEY

1. Night systems sensor scanner.
2. Pilot's Night Vision Sensor (PNVS) infra-red scanner.
3. Electro-optical target designation and night sensor systems turret.
4. Target aquisition and designation sight daylight scanner (TADS).
5. Azimuth motor housing.
6. TADS/PNVS swivelling turret.
7. Turret drive motor housing.
8. Sensor turret mounting.
9. Rear view mirror.
10. Nose compartment access hatches.
11. Remote terminal unit.
12. Signal data converter.
13. Co-pilot/gunner's yaw control rudder pedals.
14. Forward radar warning antenna.
15. M230A1 Chain Gun barrel.
16. Fuselage sponson fairing.
17. Avionics cooling air ducting.
18. Boron armoured cockpit flooring.
19. Co-pilot/gunner's 'fold-down' control column.
20. Weapons control panel.
21. Instrument panel shroud.
22. Windscreen wiper.
23. Co-Pilot/gunner's armoured windscreen.
24. Head-down sighting system viewfinder.
25. Pilot's armoured windscreen panel.
26. Windscreen wiper.
27. Co-pilot/gunner's Kevlar armoured seat.
28. Safety harness.
29. Side console panel.
30. Engine power levers.
31. Avionics equipment bays, port and starboard.
32. Avionics bay access door.
33. Collective pitch control lever.
34. Adjustable crash-resistant seat mountings.
35. Pilot's rudder pedals.
36. Cockpit side window panel.
37. Pilot's instrument console.
38. Inter-cockpit acrylic blast shield.
39. Starboard side window entry hatches.
40. Rocket launcher pack.
41. Starboard wing stores pylons.
42. Cockpit roof glazing.
43. Instrument panel shroud.
44. Pilot's Kevlar armoured seat.
45. Collective pitch control lever.
46. Side console panel.
47. Engine power levers.
48. Rear cockpit floor level.
49. Main undercarriage shock absorber mounting.
50. Linkless ammunition feed chute.
51. Forward fuel tank; total fuel capacity 375 US gal (1,419l).
52. Control rod linkages.
53. Cockpit ventilating air louvres.
54. Display adjustment panel.

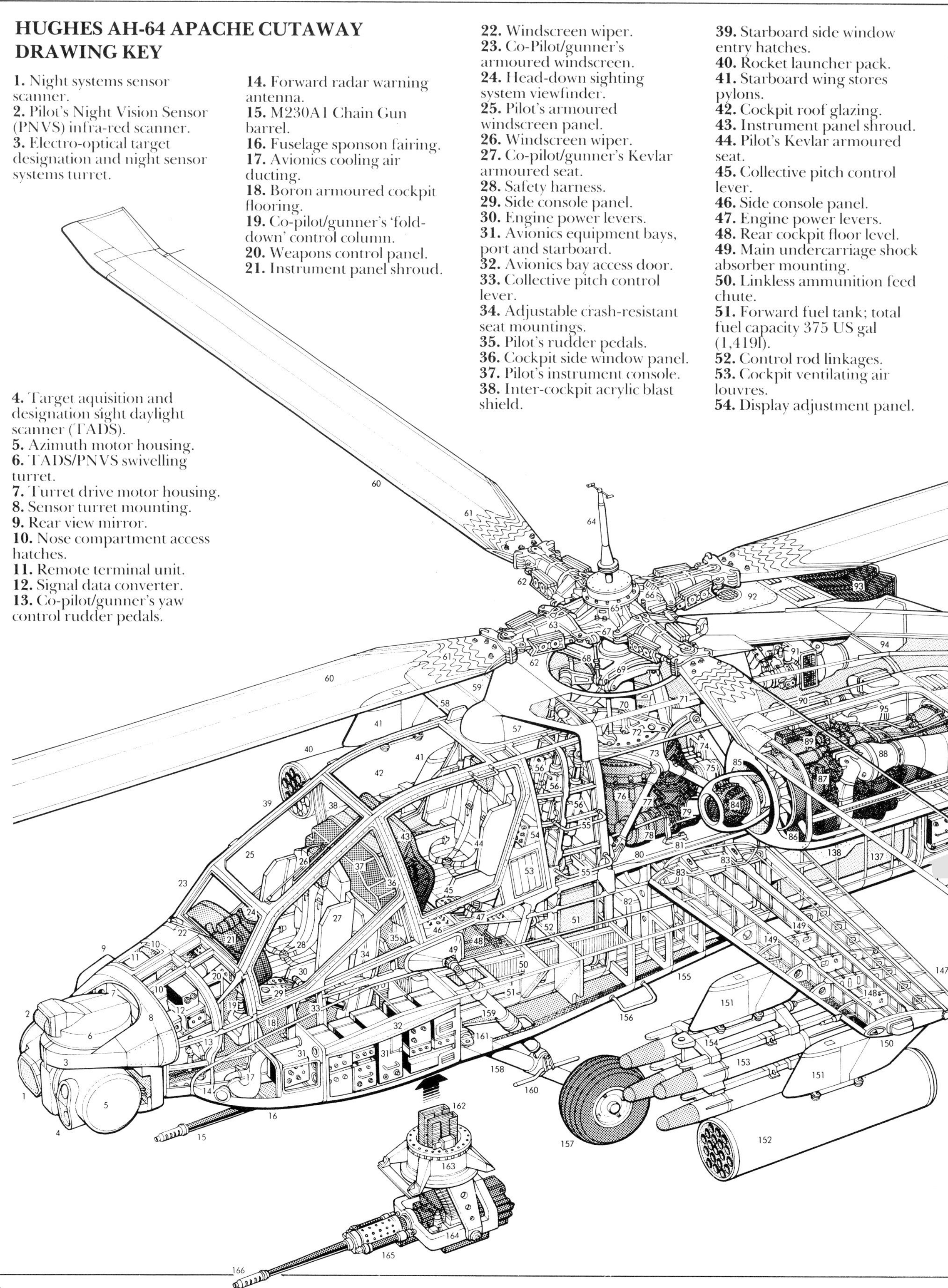

55. Grab handles/maintenance steps.
56. Control system hydraulic actuators (three).
57. Ventilating air intake.
58. UHF aerial.
59. Starboard stub wing.
60. Main rotor blades.
61. Laminated blade-root attachment joints.
62. Vibration absorbers.
63. Blade pitch bearing housing.
64. Air data sensor mast.
65. Rotor hub unit.
66. Offset flapping hinges.
67. Elastomeric lead/lag dampers.
68. Blade pitch control rod.
69. Pitch control swashplate.
70. Main rotor mast.
71. Air turbine starter/ auxiliary power unit (APU) input shaft.
72. Rotor head control mixing linkages.
73. Gearbox mounting plate.
74. Transmission oil coolers, port and starboard.
75. Rotor brake.
76. Main gearbox.
77. Gearbox mounting struts.
78. Generator.
79. Input shaft from port engine.
80. Gearbox mounting deck.
81. Tail rotor control rod linkage.
82. Ammunition magazine, 1,200 rounds.
83. Stub wing attachment joints.
84. Engine transmission gearbox.
85. Air intake.
86. Engine integral oil tank.
87. General Electric T700-GE-701 turboshaft.
88. Intake particle separator.
89. Engine accessory equipment gearbox.
90. Oil cooler plenum.
91. Gas turbine starter/ auxiliary power unit.
92. Starboard engine cowling panels/fold-down maintenance platform.
93. Starboard engine exhaust ducts.
94. APU exhaust.
95. Pneumatic system and environmental control equipment.
96. Cooling air exhaust louvres.
97. Particle separator exhaust duct/mixer.
98. 'Black Hole' infra-red suppression engine exhaust ducts.
99. Hydraulic reservoir.
100. Gearbox/engine bay tail fairings.
101. Internal maintainance platform.
102. Tail rotor control rod.
103. Spine shaft housing.
104. Tail rotor transmission shaft.
105. Shaft bearings and couplings.
106. Bevel drive intermediate gearbox.
107. Fin/rotor pylon construction.
108. Tail rotor drive shaft.
109. All moving tailplane.
110. Tail rotor gearbox housing.
111. Right-angle final drive gearbox.
112. Fin tip aerial fairing.
113. Rear radar warning antenae.
114. Tail navigation light.
115. Cambered trailing edge section (directional stability).
116. Tail rotor pitch control actuator.
117. Tail rotor hub mechanism.
118. Assymetric (noise attenuation) tail rotor blades.
119. Tailplane construction.
120. Tailplane pivot bearing.
121. Castoring tailwheel.
122. Tailwheel shock absorber.
123. Tailwheel yoke attachment.
124. Handgrips/maintenance steps.
125. Tailplane control hydraulic jack.
126. Fin/rotor pylon attachment joint.
127. Chaff and flare dispenser.
128. Tailboom ring frames.
129. Ventral radar warning aerial.
130. Tailcone frame and stringer construction.
131. UHF aerial.
132. ADF loop aerial.
133. ADF sense aerial.
134. Access hatch.
135. Handgrips/maintenance steps.
136. Radio and electronics equipment bay.
137. Rear fuel tank.
138. Reticulated foam fire suppressant tank bay linings.
139. VHF aerial.
140. Main rotor blade stainless steel spars (five).
141. Glass-fibre spar linings.
142. Honeycomb trailing edge panel.
143. Glass-fibre blade skins.
144. Trailing edge fixed tab.
145. Swept blade tip fairing.
146. Static discharger.
147. Stub wing trailing-edge flap.
148. Stub wing rib construction.
149. Twin spar booms.
150. Port navigation and strobe lights.
151. Port wing stores pylons (7cm).
152. Rocket pack: nineteen 2.75in (7cm) FFAR rockets.
153. Rockwell Hellfire AGM-114A anti-tank missiles.
154. Missile launch rails.
155. Fuselage sponson aft fairing.
156. Boarding step.
157. Port mainwheel.
158. Main undercarriage leg strut.
159. Shock absorber strut.
160. Boarding steps.
161. Main undercarriage leg pivot fixing.
162. Ammunition feed and cartridge case return chutes.
163. Gun swivelling mounting.
164. Azimuth control mounting frame.
165. Hughes M230A-1 Chain Gun 30mm automatic cannon
166. Blast suppression cannon muzzle.

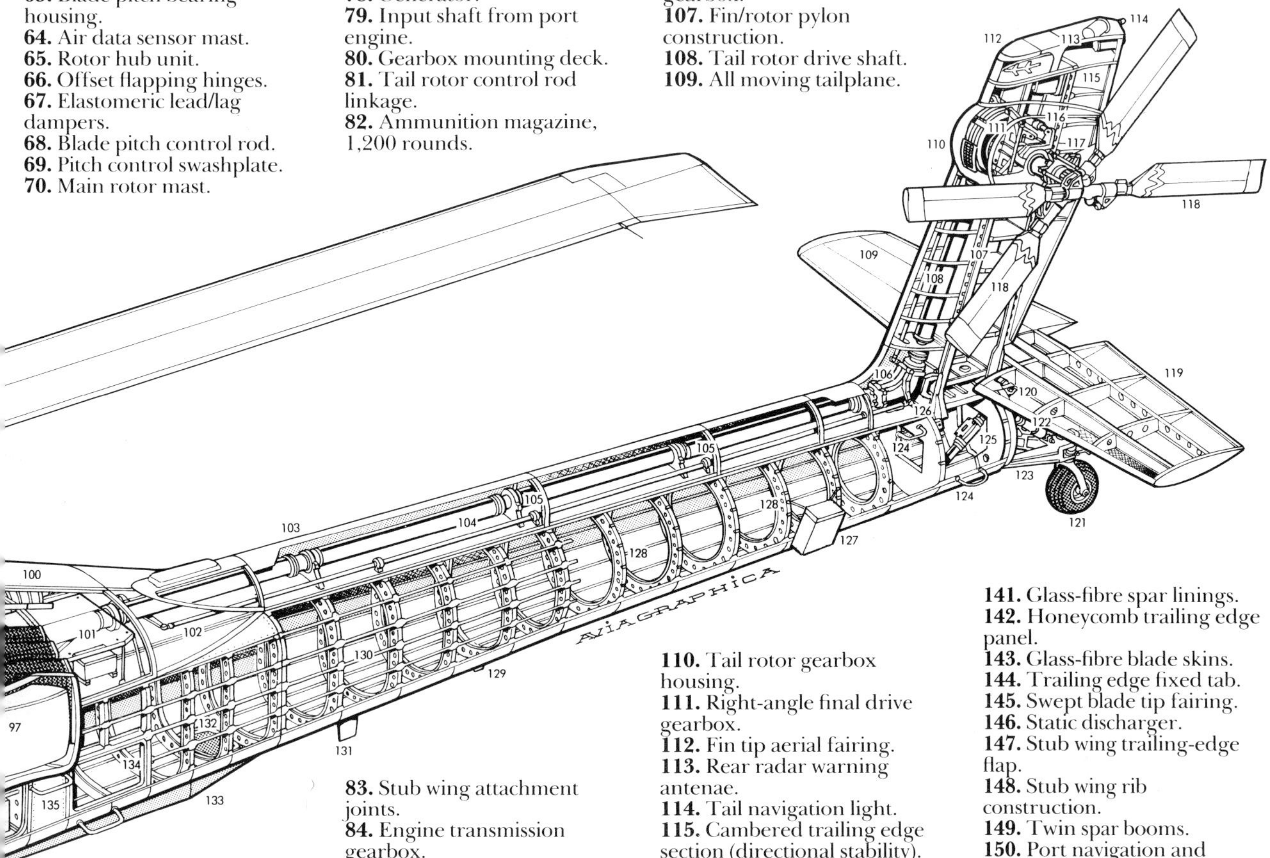

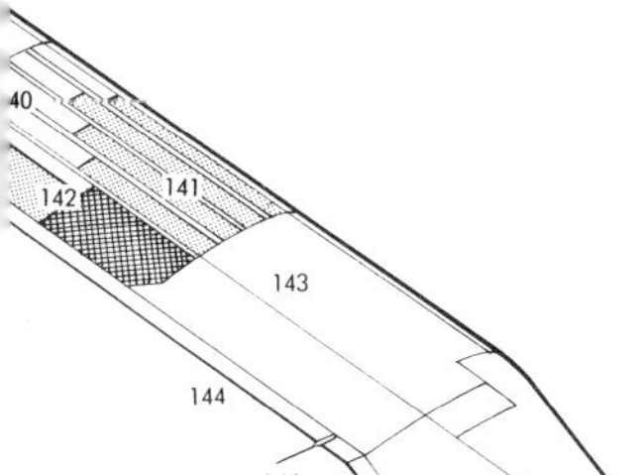

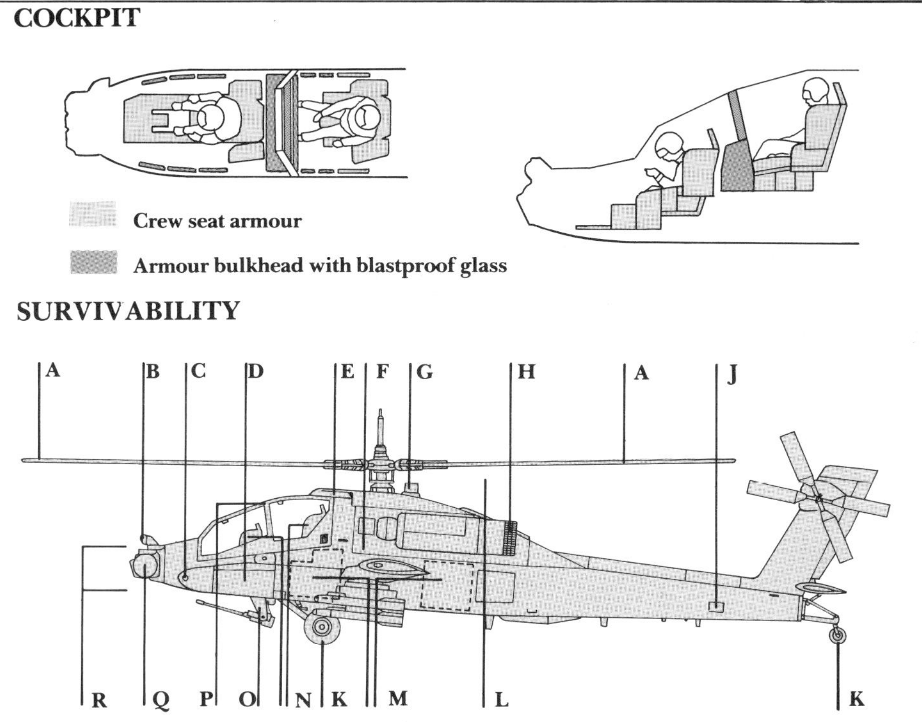

Right: The Apache cockpit is better protected than that of any previous attack helicopter. Plan and side elevations show the armoured crew seats, the blast/fragment shields around and between the cockpits and the transparent blast shield. All armour tends to be heavy, and too much eats severely into the weapon payload capacity and fuel tankage.

Right: A, low-flicker rotor; B, protected sensors; C, radar warning receiver; D, radar jammer; E, radar jammer receiver; F, ballistically tolerant structure; G, IRCM jammer; H, IR suppressed jetpipes; J, chaff/flare dispenser; K, load-absorbing collapsible landing gear; L, low aural signature; M, crash-resistant fuel cells (front and rear); N, armoured special crew seats; O, gun and mounting collapses upwards; P, strong canopy frame shaped to have a rollbar effect to protect crew; Q, recessed and protected sensors; R, load-absorbing structure.

BUCS—back-up control system—of the FBW (fly-by-wire) type. This is much lighter, can be electrically checked for integrity before each flight, and gives perfectly smooth flight with a much higher level of safety than possible with a conventional flight control system.

All primary flight controls are actuated by the Parker Hannifin (Bertea Division) dual hydraulic systems operating at 3,000lb/sq in (211kg/cm^2). The BUCS operates through the electromechanical valves on the flight-control actuators—three on the main rotor spiders, one on the tail rotor and one on the stabilator—and also makes use of the DASE (digital automatic stabilization equipment) which, like BUCS itself, is produced by Sperry. In normal operation the DASE accepts signals from stabilizing gyros, from the air-data system and from the pilot's control inputs. It improves all aspects of the Apache's flying qualities by adding damping, refining the co-ordinates of turns, tailoring all inputs and providing an attitude-hold and a hover position relative to the ground whenever the pilot requests it.

If the primary mechanical system is severed or jammed by hostile fire, the BUCS is engaged automatically. Should this occur, the DASE takes an electrical signal from a special LVDT (linear variable differential transformer) in the cockpit, processes the signal, and sends it to the control actuator. The latter responds to the LVDT input, enabling the pilot to fly the helicopter.

Fault detection and location

An equally complex and fundamental on-board system is the FD/LS (fault detection and location system), which monitors all the on-board electronic systems. The latter are to be found all over the helicopter, but most are packaged into the big bays along the left and right sides of the nose. Every functioning part is tied into the basic digital mutiplex bus, a kind of ring-main distribution and control system which handles the transfer of every bit of information. This is a part of the FCC (fire-control computer) subsystem described in the next two chapters. The FD/LS operates all the time in a continuous self-checking mode. Every on-board item is subjected to frequent automatic comparison between its real performance and its ideal performance as represented by mathematical representations.

Virtually every avionic item is boxed in a modular form, removable in seconds even by maintenance personnel wearing fur mittens. Each box, called an

Above: Line maintenance on a US Army Apache, showing the excellent all-round access to the reliable T700 engines. Most of the bulk of the cowls is taken up by the IR suppressed jetpipes.

LRU (line-replaceable unit), can be identified instantly by the FD/LS should a fault occur. In the air various measures can be taken, often automatically, to circumvent the failed unit, and a warning caption or light will illuminate in either or both cockpits. On return to base the faulty LRU can simply be unplugged and a serviceable replacement put in. Future Apaches will have even better FD/LS systems, using VHSIC (very high speed integrated circuit) technology, while FD/LS data will also be interlinked with on-board maintenance recorders for improved interactive participation by operating and maintenance crews.

All attack helicopters need an accurate system to measure true airspeed, drift and air density, and possibly other parameters also. This is needed in order to aim weapons correctly, even though the helicopter will probably not be travelling in the exact direction it is pointing. On the prototype Apaches the air-data sensors were on a boom projecting from the left avionic bay. The ADSS (air-data subsystem) in the production helicopter is the responsibility of Pacer Systems, and apart from a large LRU in one of the avionics bays the main item is the small mast on top of the main rotor. This carries lateral arms bearing air-data sensors at the tips. These transmit electrical signals representing omnidirectional and exact air data over the entire flight envelope. The outputs are passed not only to the displays in both cockpits but also to the FCC (fire-control computer) for the computation of complex mathematics for rocket launching and for first-round hits with the gun. Other signals go to the stabilator actuator computer, stability augmentation computer and navigational doppler for Earth-wind computation.

Three engines

Of course, the source of on-board power comes from the gas-turbine engines, and in fact there are three. The main engines, used for propulsion, are the T700s mounted outside the fuselage and driving through a nose gearbox on each side. Each engine comprises a gas-generator, or core, with axial and centrifugal compressors driven by a two-stage air-cooled gas-generator turbine, and a central shaft to the nose output gearbox driven by a two-stage LP (low-pressure) power turbine. At the front is the heated inlet which incorporates an automatic integral particle separator. This has no moving parts and relies on the tendency of particles to carry on in straight lines while the air is sucked sharply inwards to enter the axial compressor. About 95 per cent of ingested sand, dust, salt and other material is automatically removed and dumped overboard by a blower driven by the engine accessory gearbox. The resulting intensely "dirty" airflow is blown into the side of the IR-suppressed exhaust compartment.

Auxiliary power unit

The third engine is the Garrett GTP36-55(H) APU (auxiliary power unit). Situated slightly higher up between the main engines, aft of the rotor mast, the APU is rated at 125shp (93kW), and provides compressed air for starting the main engines and electricity for maintenance checking. The main engines are identical, and not handed left or right, and each has its own self-contained lubricating oil and ignition system. Fuel is housed in two crash-resistant cells in the fuselage, one ahead of the rotor and the other about the same distance aft, with a combined capacity of 313gal (376 US gal, 1,422 litres). For ferrying, four Kevlar auxiliary underwing tanks can add another 920 US gal, but no inflight-refuelling probe is provided for.

Hughes (now McDonnell Douglas Helicopters) itself developed the Black Hole IR suppression system for the engine jetpipes. Even a modest turboshaft engine pumps out more than enough heat to serve as a target for a modern IR sensor or seeker head, and a hot jetpipe could form a particularly "juicy" target. There is no possibility of reducing the heat output, which depends entirely on engine power, but there is much that can be done to shield all hot metal and cool the jet exhaust. In the Black Hole system fresh air is continuously drawn in to a large mixer compartment. There are no moving parts, the pumping action being affected by the jets themselves. The cold air mixes with the jets, and all an enemy can "see" are cool plumes of gas/air mixture emerging from large boxes without a single spot hot enough to trigger an IR seeker. In addition the external skin of even slightly warm areas is coated with special IR paint, resulting in extremely low signatures right across the spectrum of wavelengths.

Below: The T700 engine is dominated by the giant pipe passing upwards amidships and ending in the aft-facing ejector for ingested dirt. The inlet is at the left, jetpipe at the right.

3
Apache Sensors

FROM LONG before the launch of the AAH programme it has been evident that sensors would play a crucial and central role. In the little Bell Sioux Scout there had been no sensors. Partly because of payload limitations, the small helicopter had carried little mission equipment beyond communications radio and an optical sight. Unfortunately, this was enough for it to fly quite useful missions in clear daytime conditions: it has become a truism to state that US airpower has been gravely damaged by the sunshine and blue skies of California, Nevada, Arizona and New Mexico. Fortunately, the AAH was specifically created in order to provide better defence against the armour of the Warsaw Pact powers, and these vehicles could be expected to roll Westwards in a mixture of rain, snow, fog and night.

Nap of the Earth flying

From the outset it was recognized that the AAH had to have a crew of two. Even with the workload shared, the task of flying the mission is a daunting one. It is necessary to fly NOE (nap of the Earth), which means heights much lower than the "low level" attack by a fast jet. There has to be a relationship between NOE height and the helicopter's speed; the Apache can fly at 200mph (322km/h), and at such a speed it is not possible to follow every undulation of broken ground, dodge round trees and skim over or under the wires and cables that cover Northern Europe. In fog, smoke and other conditions of bad visibility the safe speed has to be brought very low. In due course VHSIC (very high speed integrated-circuit) technology will make possible a largely automated single-seat helicopter, with avionics and sensors that will permit sustained operation at the highest speed the pilot wishes while always protecting it against collision with the ground or anything projecting up from it. The new LHX programme is aiming to get very near this capability, but the Apache still needs to be flown manually, though with the help of a lot of useful "black boxes".

This chapter is concerned mainly with the sensors that supplement the eyes and ears of the crew in the primary task of killing hostile armour. Such targets are small, highly mobile, and can be found almost anywhere. They are certain to be as well hidden or camouflaged as possible—though they are much more visible when on the march across country or even along highways—and they will always be protected by frightening concentrations of triple-A (anti-aircraft artillery, notably the ZSU-23-4 four-barrel

Below: The sensors on a production AH-64A Apache comprise the multisensor TADS below and the simpler pilot's PNVS above. All sensors are complementary and there is a degree of redundancy.

23mm amphibious vehicle) and SAMs (surface-to-air missiles, all of them again carried on amphibious armoured vehicles). The helicopter thus has to try to see without being seen. The Apache was designed to be able to survive even a burst of radar-aimed fire from a ZSU-23-4, but there was no way it could be made to survive interception by SAMs. At present, like the vulnerability of airfields to instant elimination by missiles, this is a problem swept under the collective US carpet as being too difficult to solve.

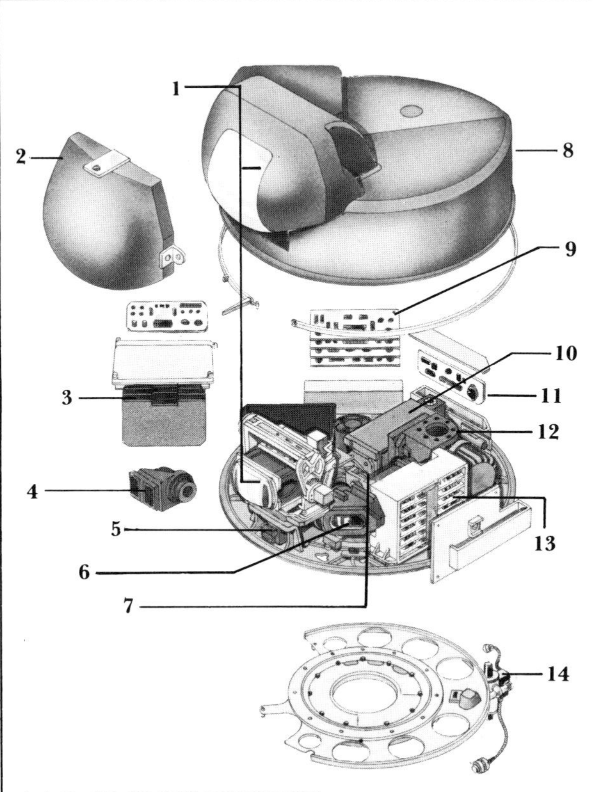

AAQ–11 PNVS TURRET

Above: The PNVS (Pilot's Night Vision Sensor) serves the backseat pilot only. It incorporates a sensitive FLIR (forward-looking infra-red) sensor. Key: 1, Elevation mirror and afocal lens. 2, Window cover. 3, Post amplifier control driver. 4, LED/collimator assembly. 5, Azimuth gyroscope. 6, Infra-red imager. 7, Focussing mechanism. 8, Shroud. 9, Power regulator. 10, Visual relay multiplexer. 11, Focus control. 12, Cool/dewar assembly. 13, Video IR preamplifier. 14, Azimuth drive gimbal.

Sensors grouped in nose

What is perhaps much more curious is that, from the start of the AAH programme, the main sensors have been grouped in the nose. This location rules out any possibility of seeing without being seen. To watch the enemy, or fire at him, the Apache crew have to expose the whole helicopter to view (except in the special case of firing Hellfire missiles blindly from behind a hill against a laser-designated target). This is clearly a serious disadvantage, and it is not much of an answer to point to the Apache's ability to withstand hostile fire. As already noted, SAMs could fireball the whole machine in an instant, and a single bullet could kill the pilot.

When the full-scale engineering development of the Hughes helicopter was ordered, on 10 December 1976, the contract also required the development of a visionics system—an electronic aid to finding and hitting targets—capable of being used at night or in

SENSORS AT WORK

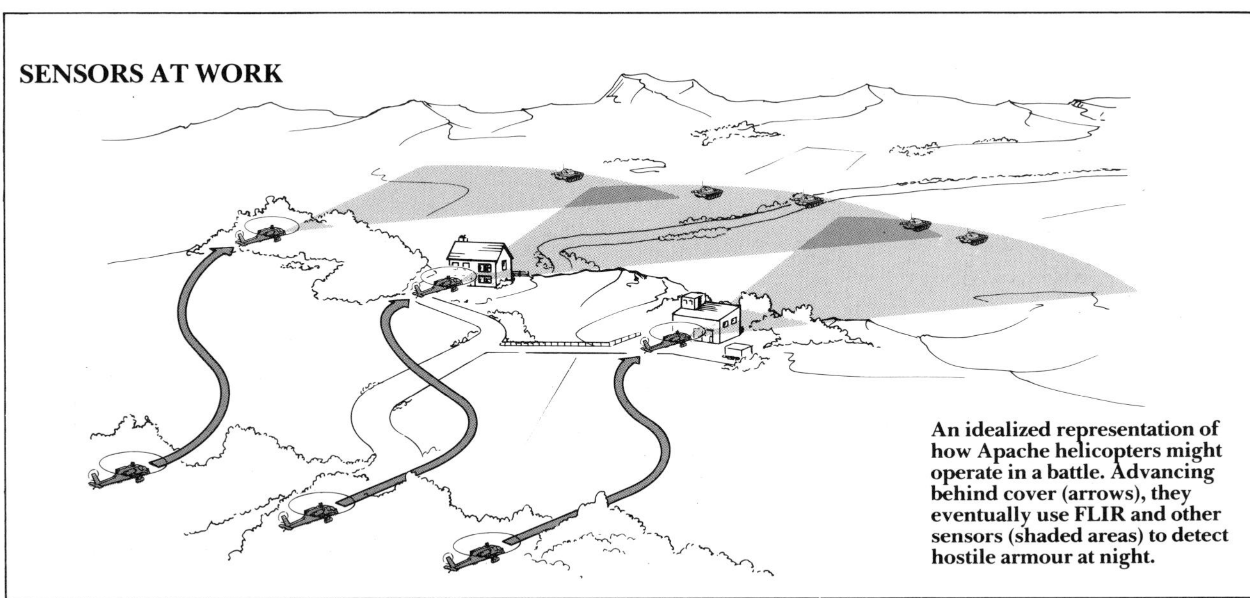

An idealized representation of how Apache helicopters might operate in a battle. Advancing behind cover (arrows), they eventually use FLIR and other sensors (shaded areas) to detect hostile armour at night.

bad weather, as well as the fire-control equipment necessary to integrate this system with both the area weapon and the anti-tank weapon, as described in the next chapter. Previously all that had been known for certain was that the new helicopter would need a stabilized optical sight offering varying degrees of target magnification, some form of precise target-ranging system, a means of seeing targets at night and probably a laser (certainly a receiver and probably a transmitter) for use in connection with laser-guided weapons, again as described in the next chapter.

The reason for putting the sensors in the nose was only partly to give them the best possible field of view. The overriding factor was that guns are much less expensive than sensors, and in a typical crash landing whatever is underneath is likely to be crushed and whatever is inside the nose is likely to survive. As for the much better location of an MMS (mast-mounted sight), which according to current evaluations by four nations gives from eight to 12 times less likelihood of being shot down, this was in its infancy in 1976, and the Army was anxious to move quickly and minimize risk. In the author's view not yet shared by everyone in the Army—an MMS would have had a much better chance of being selected if it had been realised that getting the Apache into combat service was going to take not the planned 56 months but another ten years.

By 1977 it had been decided to split the visionics into two main installations, called the TADS (target acquisition designation sight) and the PNVS (pilot's

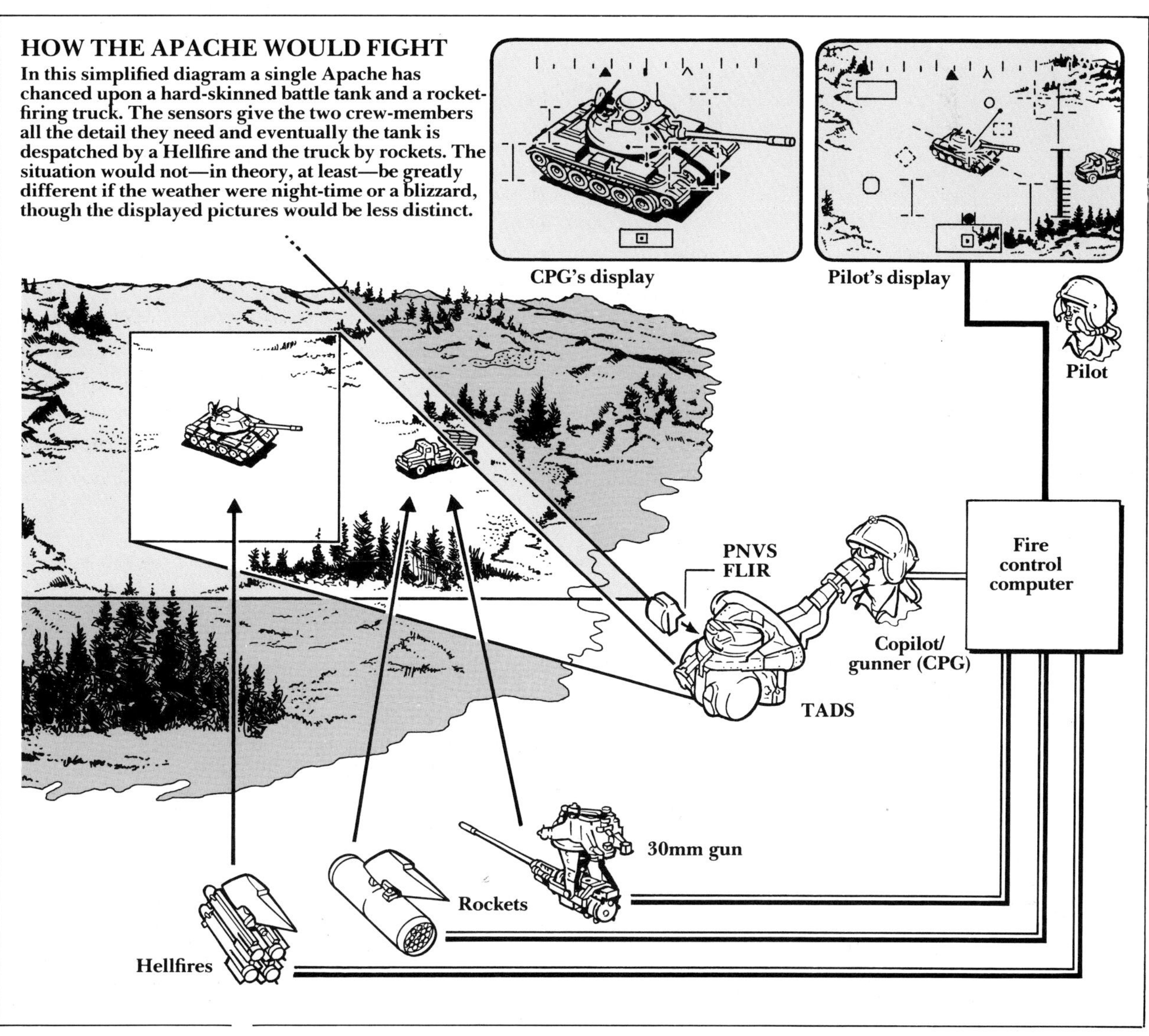

HOW THE APACHE WOULD FIGHT
In this simplified diagram a single Apache has chanced upon a hard-skinned battle tank and a rocket-firing truck. The sensors give the two crew-members all the detail they need and eventually the tank is despatched by a Hellfire and the truck by rockets. The situation would not—in theory, at least—be greatly different if the weather were night-time or a blizzard, though the displayed pictures would be less distinct.

Above: In typical "hull down" position an Apache is hard to see or destroy. But as it has no mast-mounted sight, it is blind and impotent here until it exposes itself.

night-vision system). Competitive development was put in hand with two possible contractors for the complete system, Martin Marietta and Northrop's Electro-Mechanical Division at Anaheim. In the same way the associated missile, Hellfire, was the result of competitive development by Rockwell and Hughes (Hughes Aircraft, not Helicopters).

TADS "bug eyes" impression

As previously noted, prototypes AV02 and 03 resumed their flight programmes at the end of 1978, the former with the Northrop sensors and 03 with the Martin Marietta installation. The noses of the two machines were visibly different. Northrop got off the mark first, not only with the first flight of the upgraded 02 but also in launching (unguided) Hellfires in spring 1979 and in autonomous Hellfire shots using the TADS in October of that year. It was to no avail, because in April 1980 the choice fell on the Martin Marietta product.

The Apache's sensors have sometimes been described as "like bug eyes". In fact the impression is due solely to the TADS, which occupies what looks like a big oil drum fixed transversely under the nose. The impression is startling, and it is doubtful if any of man's weapons has ever looked so much like a menacing living monster as an attacking Apache—though it looks a bit cross-eyed, one "eye" being orange-yellow and the other purple-blue! The PNVS is relatively unobtrusive, being the small turret on top.

Of the two sensor units, PNVS is much the simpler. Mounted in its turret above the nose, it can sweep to 90° to left or right, while tilted to any angle from 20° above the horizontal (relative to the helicopter) to 45° down. Slew rate is up to 120° per second. Field of view is 30° × 40°, which gives a diagonal FOV of 50°. The PNVS contains an AAQ-11 Mk III IR sensor operating in the far-infrared range at wavelengths of 8 to 14 microns (a micron is a millionth of a metre or a thousandth of a millimetre). Like all such sensors the AAQ-11 incorporates a focussing mechanism, cryogenic dewar (vacuum flask) to refrigerate the sensitive cell to a very low temperature to eliminate unwanted "noise" from the background, an azimuth gyro, and various am-

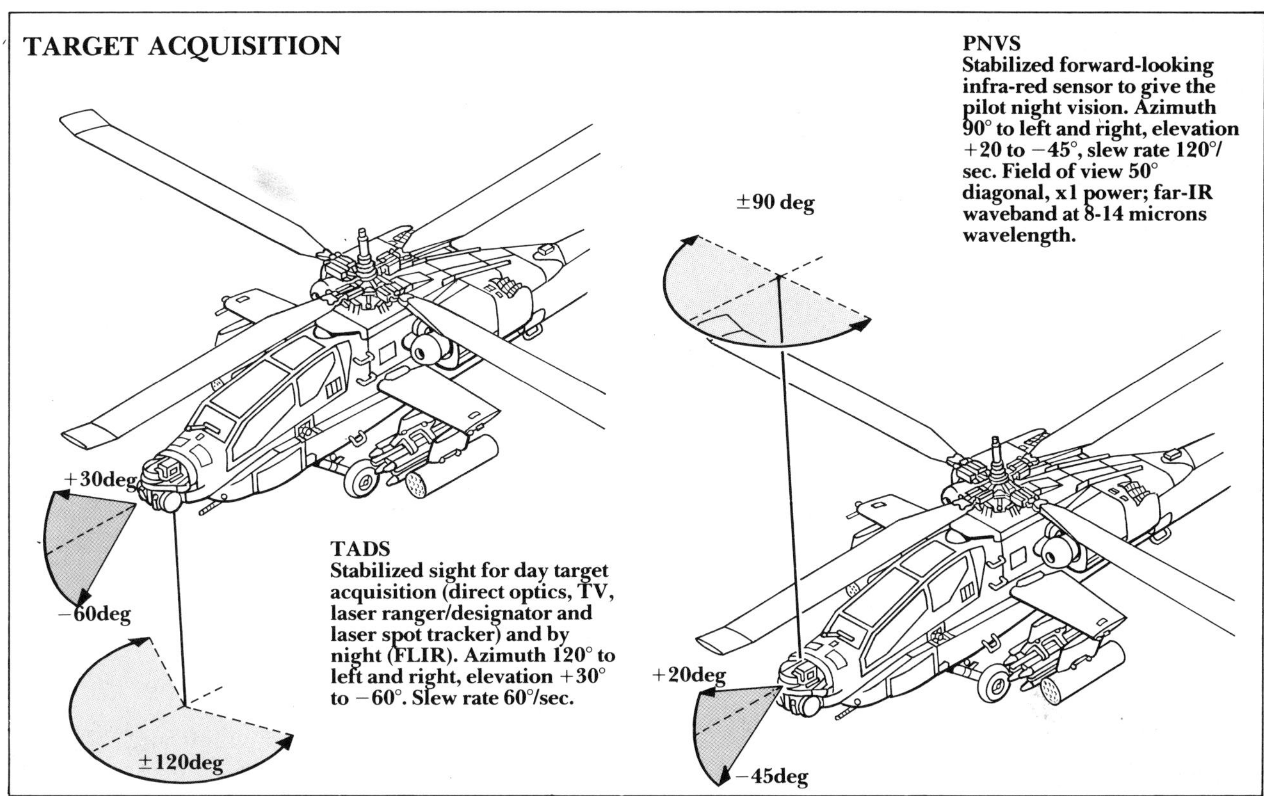

plifiers, power relays and multiplexers. The result is a signal in video (TV) form which is passed to the fire-control computer into the Honeywell Avionics IHADSS (integrated helmet and display sighting subsystem), which is a monocle display in front of one eye of the wearer of a special helmet. In fact, both crew-members wear these special helmets, though normally only the pilot has IHADSS imagery in action.

Thermal imaging

The IHADSS is electronically slaved to the PNVS, so that the latter "looks" wherever the pilot is looking. The picture it presents, focussed in front of the pilot's eye (usually the right eye), is a bright monochrome picture of the scene at which the pilot is looking, neither reduced nor magnified, and totally unaffected by the blackest night, rain, smoke or other obscuration. As it is a thermal picture, it records scene temperature variations; warm targets such as vehicles, people or any other heat source stand out brightly (usually white, but polarity can be reversed to give black targets against a cooler white background).

In addition to the basic PNVS picture the IHADSS also presents the pilot with a great deal of other vital information in the form of alphanumerics (letters and numbers) and bright symbols or lines. The "menu" of information varies according to whether the helicopter is in the cruise regime, or in transition to slower NOE flight, or in the hover, or in the bob-up manoeuvre to fire at the enemy, the regime being selected by a four-position switch on the pilot's cyclic stick. For example, in cruising flight the IHADSS adds a heading scale across the top of the PNVS picture, showing current heading and desired heading; a digital altitude display, plus an expanded altitude strip which appears the instant height above ground falls below 200ft (91m); a rate of climb indication; a diamond-shaped aircraft symbol, horizon line and sideslip display; digital readout of airspeed and engine torque (a direct indication of power); PNVS line-of-sight reticle, shown in the standard crosshair arrangement; and, when the sight selector is in the PNVS position, the PNVS gimbal limits.

When the Apache slows for NOE flight, the "transition" symbols can be switched in. These protect the helicopter in slow flight below the treetops, providing different cruise symbology: a velocity vector consisting of a heavy straight line with a black disc at the end extending from the PNVS reticle to indicate the direction and rate of aircraft movement, and an acceleration cursor in the form of a small circle to provide the pilot with predicted magnitude and direction of movement. Selection of the "hover" mode erases the horizon line and increases the sensitivity of the velocity vector and acceleration cursor so that any drift from the desired hovering position will be indicated immediately.

All this information, as well as TADS imagery, can also be displayed on the VSD (vertical situation display) or video display unit which dominates the pilot's panel. PNVS information can also be supplied to the CPG in the front cockpit, especially should the pilot be incapacitated and the CPG have to take over the flying.

Five sensors of TADS

Normally the CPG concentrates on the TADS, which is a bigger and much more complicated installation incorporating five sensors: DVO (direct-view optics), DTV (day television), LRF/D (laser rangefinder and designator, LST (laser spot tracker) and FLIR (forward-looking infrared). The first four sensors form the TADS daylight sensor and occupy the left portion (as seen by the crew) of the large barrel container under the nose. The FLIR forms the night sensor and occupies the right, or starboard, portion. The whole installation, called a turret, slews at up to 60° per second in azimuth to limits at no less than 120° to left or right, and rotates to an elevation of 30° above the helicopter's horizontal axis and 60° below. As its name suggests, the TADS is used chiefly to find targets, lock-on to them, determine range and bearing and also provide laser designation. It can operate at night, and has limited all-weather capability though range is limited by rain, snow and similar obscuration when using the FLIR as the day adverse-weather sensor. It is a matter of cost-effectiveness, and TADS is still regarded as the best that can be done for an attack helicopter using current technology and at an affordable price.

The DTV and DVO share a common boresight, looking through the same optics in the left (bluish-coloured) windows in the TADS turret. The optical sight has two settings, a ×3.5 magnification with a wide (18°) field of view, and a ×16 magnification with a narrow (4°) FOV. Obviously the wide field is used when searching for targets and the high-power magnification for studying targets and guiding ordnance. The TV has three modes, a wide-FOV of 4°, a narrow-FOV of 0.9° and an underscan mode with a pencil beam of 0.45°. According to weather conditions the CPG can use direct optics or, in conditions of bad weather or battlefield smoke, he can use the TV, which operates in the near-infrared. At night he switches in the FLIR which, in order to have the highest possible "seeing capability" and definition in heavy precipitation or high humidity, has the largest available aperture of 9in (229mm). If necessary it can back up the PNVS, its picture being relayed to the same IHADSS monocle and pilot panel display.

The laser sensors in the TADS are both directly concerned with targeting and the precision delivery of missiles. The LST is a passive receiver tuned to the emissions of friendly laser designators which can be aimed at targets by ground troops or other aircraft. It automatically detects and locks-on to the emission from such designated targets, and passes the target data to the IHADSS, cockpit displays and weapon-aiming avionics. The International Laser Systems LRF/D is, in contrast, an active laser, aimed by the CPG via the TADS turret at selected targets. It thus can designate targets for the Apache's own Hellfire missiles, or for Hellfires fired in remote attacks by other helicopters hiding behind natural cover, or for Copperhead laser-homing shells fired by friendly artillery.

Interchange of information

The TADS system includes, in addition to the turret, three avionics boxes in the main avionics bays, an ORT (optical relay tube) in the CPG's front cockpit, and various cockpit controls and displays. A diagram shows the main two-handed MSS (multipurpose sight system) used by the CPG to aim sensors and weapons, control the TADS and night vision and select gun, missiles or rockets. Though the TADS and PNVS are individual systems, each normally controlled by the CPG and pilot respectively, there is full provision for interchange of information between the cockpits and for transfer of control if necessary. For example, either crew-member can spot a target, take charge and, by merely looking straight at the target through his IHADSS, cue his partner and weapons to aim at that exact spot.

Other on-board avionics include the LDNS (light-weight doppler navigation system) and HARS (heading/attitude reference system for precision navigation in NOE flight and for storing target locations, a standard radio ADF (auto direction finder) relying on ground stations, secure UHF/AM, VHF/AM and FM communications radio, and a lightweight IFF transponder with a secure encoding

Below and right: The AAQ-11 PNVS presents the pilot with a clear black/white monochrome picture which is actually a plot of surface temperatures. Superimposed on it are guidance lines and numerical symbology. All the information can be supplied to the IHADSS (integrated helmet and display sighting system) shown in use below.

feature. Combat survivability is greatly increased by comprehensive inbuilt EW (electronic warfare) and IRCM systems. The RWR (radar warning receiver) is the Loral APR-39(V), which is served by two passive spiral helix aerials (antennas) facing diagonally outward from the front of the two main avionics bays. Two more receivers could be added to cover the rear. This system provides automatic warning of illumination by almost all likely hostile radars, giving both visual and aural warnings, and indications of bearing, identity and radar operating modes.

In the left avionics bay is the ITT ALQ-136(V)1 which, under microprocessor control, pumps out powerful jamming in the I/J bands from a transmitting aerial in the top of the nose. The associated radar jammer receiver aerial is in the top of the fuselage aft of the cockpit. Further back, immediately aft of the rotor mast, is the dustbin-like beacon of the Sanders ALQ-144 IRCM (infrared countermeasures) set. This houses an electrically heated ceramic brick which forms a brilliantly powerful source of IR radiation, whose emissions are modulated by computer-controlled shutters in the surrounding structure to confuse the seeker head of an oncoming missile and cause it to break lock. Space/weight/power provisions are also made for an AVR-2 LWR (laser warning receiver) above the root of the left wing. To give protection against hostile radars throughout a mission (the ALQ-136 being switched on only during the bob-up manoeuvre) chaff can be dispensed from the Tracor M-130 system, which ejects standard chaff (or flare) cartridges from boxes on each side near the rear of the tailboom. Each box holds 30 payloads, each 1in (25mm) square and 8.25in (210mm) in length.

Below: The business end of a fully combat-ready Apache, armed with AGM-114A Hellfire missiles. Even the ALQ-144 IRCM beacon is installed, immediately behind main rotor hub.

Above: This is approximately the view ahead enjoyed by an Apache CPG (copilot/gunner). Unusually, he sits under a roof which slopes sharply down to meet a shallow bullet-proof windshield, the metal canopy frame being strong enough not to crush in most severe crashes. In the centre is the main sensor/sight system for aiming Hellfire missiles and rockets.

Right: The pilot's cockpit, here viewed through the open right-hand window, is significantly higher than that of the CPG to give a clear view ahead over the Kevlar seat in the front cockpit. Between the cockpits is a thick acrylic panel impervious to bullets and splinters. This advanced pilot cockpit is having a big influence on that for the next generation LHX helicopter.

Above: This view gives a clear indication of the Apache's weapons and sensors. The PNVS (pilot's right vision sensor) above the nose is swivelled to look at the photographer, and via the IHADSS could aim the gun at him on a dark night.

Right: Head-on aspect of a standard AH-64A Apache of the US Army, carrying standard armament of four Hellfire missiles and one FFAR rocket pod on each wing. The gun is in its usual nose-up stowed position, aligned dead ahead for minimum drag.

Below: The right side elevation of the same US Army Apache. The IRCM turret, which broadcasts pulsed waves of heat to confuse missiles is mounted just behind the rotor, and the chaff/flares box is on the side of the rear fuselage.

Above: Top view of the same US Army AH-64A Apache, showing the main rotor, weapon wings, engine installations and (aft of the rotor) the IRCM turret. Note the extra width of the avionics bays built on each side of the forward fuselage.

Left: From the outset of its operational career the primary anti-tank weapon of the Apache has been the hefty Hellfire missile, one of which is here being loaded by two crew members into a lower inboard launch rail. Missile weight is 101lb.

Above: Left-hand side elevation of an AH-64A Apache fitted with the ALQ-144 IRCM turret but with no FFAR rocket launchpods outboard of the quadruple Hellfires. Nose sensors are aligned fore and aft, as they normally are when inoperative.

Above: Underside view of Army Apache configured with the normal mixed armament of gun, Hellfires and rockets. White spots on the rear fuselage ventral box are sense aerials (antennas) for the ADF (automatic radio direction finder).

Below: Left-hand side elevation of a production AH-64A Apache in the ferry configuration, with four auxiliary fuel tanks. With these in place these helicopters can deploy under their own power from the USA to Europe, though it is a long grind.

Left: Front view of the proposed Sea Apache in its original McDonnell Douglas Helicopter Company form. Weapons include AGM-84 Harpoon anti-ship cruise missiles, FFAR rockets and AIM-9L or -9M Sidewinder air-to-air missiles for self-defence.

Below: Left-side elevation of the Sea Apache as proposed to the US Navy in 1984-86. To fit ship parking spaces this version would need a folding tail and thus a forward-located tailwheel. No defense money has yet been voted for this model.

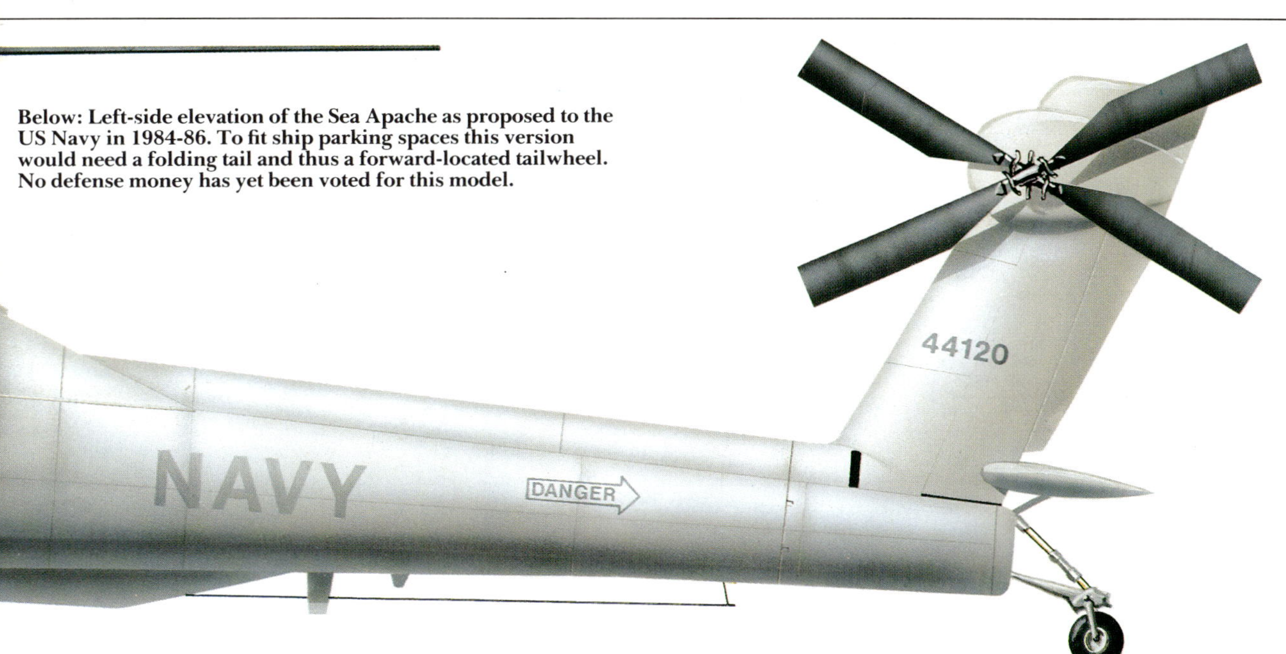

Below left: Underside view of the original proposed Sea Apache. This has never been a firm or funded programme, and—despite allegations of at least equal price—the Marines may stick with the AH-1W SuperCobra which has the same engines.

Below: Looking down from above on the baseline Sea Apache, showing the originally considered weapon mix. No IRCM turret is shown, and in fact not only the equipment fit but the very helicopter itself was highly problematical in late 1986.

Above: McDonnell Douglas Helicopter test pilots departing on a simulated long-range deployment mission in ferry configuration with four auxiliary tanks. These extend range from 260nm (482km, 300 miles) to 918nm (1,701km, 1,057 miles).

Left: The nose sensors with main TADS (target acquisition and designation sight) "looking" at the photographer. What appears to be an exhaust pipe on the right side is a rear view mirror.

Below: Two fully armed Apaches on a training mission over the desert. Note how far the main landing gears hang down when unloaded. On the ground they are soft and spongy.

4
Apache Weapons

FROM THE start of the AAH programme it was universally agreed that there would have to be two main types of weapon on board. The primary purpose of the helicopter is to kill hostile armour, and this requires a long-range missile with a heavy hollow-charge warhead and all-the-way precision guidance. For defensive suppressive fire a different kind of area weapon system is needed, and to this end the helicopter required a powerful gun and a rocket subsystem.

In the mid-1970s the obvious anti-tank missile to choose was BGM-71 TOW, tube-launched optically-tracked and wire-guided. Its only serious operating deficiency when fired from a helicopter—that it has to be optically tracked and wire-guided (by transmitting the operator's steering signals along fine wires) all the way to the target—requires that the operator, such as the CPG in the front cockpit of an Apache, should keep the enemy armoured vehicle clearly in view for anything up to 13 or 14 seconds while he steers the missile towards it. With perhaps 100 hostile AAA and SAM vehicles looking for targets this not only seems like an eternity but is (in the author's view) wholly unacceptable. The US Army wisely decided that, for the future AAH, a new missile should be developed which would free the helicopter from this long exposure.

Hellfire development

As noted earlier, Hughes Aircraft (prime contractor for TOW) and Rockwell International fought for the new missile, starting work in late 1973. The advances that could be made over all previous anti-armour weapons were considerable, embracing warhead size and lethality, guidance precision and reliability, flight speed, range, short flight time and, in most versions, the ability to plunge down from above to pierce through the thinner top skin of the target. As there was clearly something to be said for each of several guidance systems, the missile was made modular and trials were held with homing heads using laser light, TV guidance and IR homing on the heat of the target.

In October 1976 Rockwell was selected to enter FSED (full-scale engineering development) of the laser-seeking version, with designation AGM-114A Hellfire (the appropriate name coming from "helicopter-launched fire and forget". Compared with TOW it is appreciably larger and heavier, with a length of 64in (1,626mm) compared with 45.75in (1,162mm) and launch weight of 101lb (45.8kg) compared with (for TOW 1) 46.1lb (20.9kg). This

Below: An early Apache firing rockets at desert targets in 1982. Maximum load is four launchers each with 19 FFARs, a total of 76. Here the inboard pylons are occupied by Hellfires.

enables a more powerful solid-propellant rocket motor to be fittd, and its very high impulse quickly accelerates the Hellfire to about Mach 1.17 (around 890mph, 1,432km/h), appreciably faster than any other anti-tank missile in the Western world. This high speed results in short flight-times over all engagement distances, preventing the target from performing evasive manoeuvres and reducing the time the launch aircraft is exposed to counterfire.

Above: A combat-ready Apache on manoeuvres from Davison Army Airfield in 1986. Note the IRCM turret immediately aft of the main rotor. The AH-64 is climbing to engage the enemy.

Hellfire's engagement flexibility

Indeed, the launch aircraft may not be exposed to counterfire at all. Among the many original requirements for the new missile was the need for indirect fire, the launch aircraft being able to remain hidden and never coming within view of the target. In fact the engagement flexibility of Hellfire is one of the most remarkable of its advances. Autonomous designation means that the Apache itself uses its laser (LRF/D) to illuminate the target with laser light exactly coded to be compatible with its own missiles. In this case, of course, only direct fire is possible, but it is still possible to fire several missiles in rapid succession, moving the laser designation spot from one target to another to provide the required guidance during the vital terminal phase of flight. In all LOAL (lock-on after launch) modes the missile is fired in the direction of the target, often climbing to quite a high altitude provided it does not enter cloud and can always "see" the target. A laser designator then illuminates the target; the Hellfire instantly detects the radiation scattered from the target and homes on it, normally plunging down at a steep angle.

If there were 16 laser designators available, aimed by friendly ground forces or other aircraft, then an Apache could launch 16 Hellfires simultaneously. Each would eventually spot the radiation of the individual laser to which its guidance seeker was coded and immediately home on to its source. This

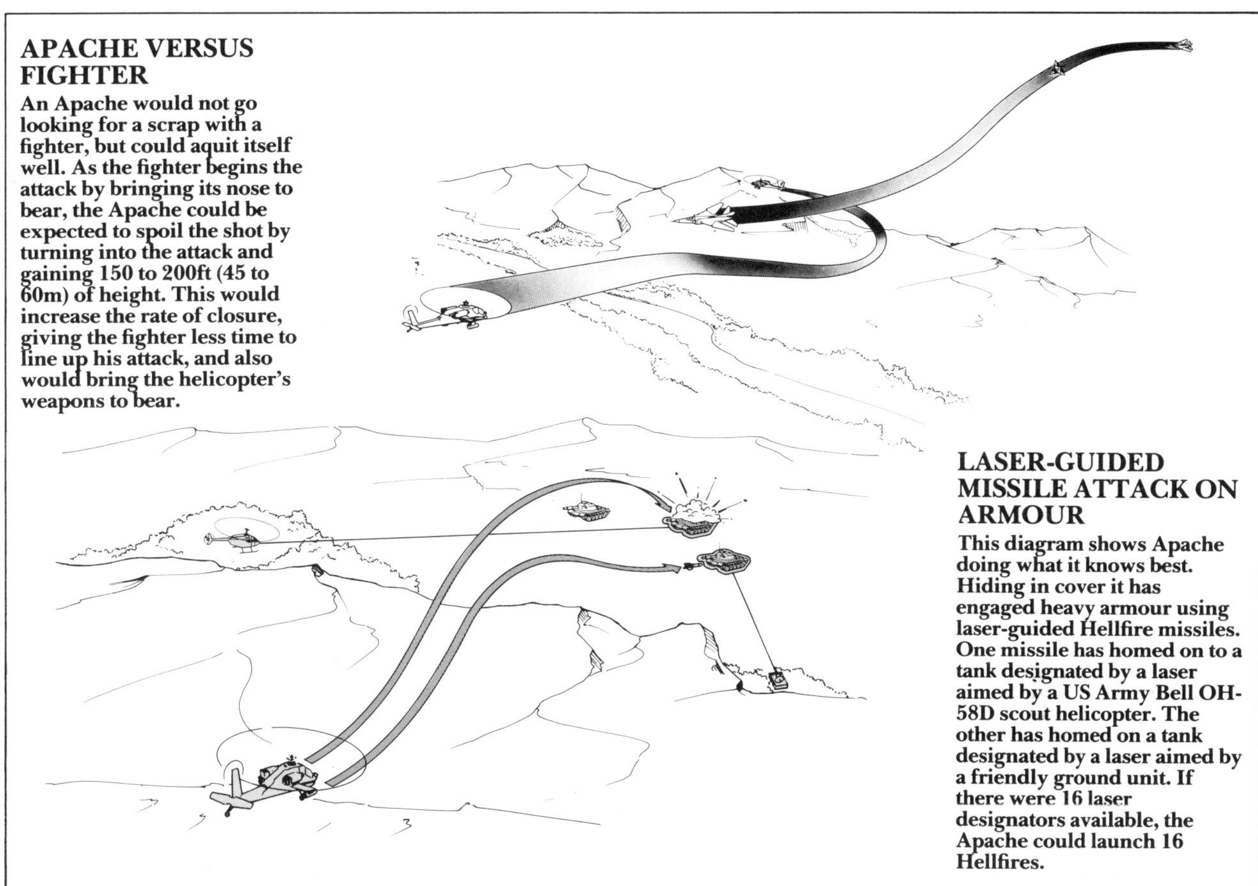

remote designation is expected to be extremely important in future, the Apaches being teamed with Bell OH-58D AHIP (Army helicopter improvement programme) scout helicopters, which are expected to stand off from the battlefield and designate targets with their lasers. They can do this much more safely than can the Apaches, because the OH-58D laser is in an MMS on a pillar high above the rotor. All the enemy might see is the spherical top of the MMS, not much bigger than a beach ball, the helicopter remaining hidden. Of course, the scout's laser beam must be exactly coded for compatibility with the Hellfire selected by the Apache CPG, or the missile will fail to recognise the vital emission coming from the reflective surfaces of the target and will fall aimlessly to one side. There must also be instantaneous, yet secure, communication between the two helicopters, which must throughout the engagement know each other's exact position. Thus, the timing must be so accurate that the Apache can fire a Hellfire a few seconds before the partner scout helicopter aims its laser exactly on target.

The vital feature of this technique is that the Apache, the costly and fully armed attack member of the team, can remain in what the troops call a "defilade" position, which means it can stay hidden behind natural ground cover. With remote designation it is possible to use either rapid (closely spaced sequence) or ripple (simultaneous salvo) fire, of any number of Hellfires up to the maximum of 16. It does, however, demand absolutely perfect teamwork. One can imagine how easy it would be to get the timing slightly wrong, or the laser coding between the designators and the missiles slightly wrong, so that (for example) each missile might home on its target until it was about 1,000ft (300m) away, at which point the laser would switch to the next target. If the targets were moving then every missile would miss.

Everyone associated with Hellfire raves about it, most of all the Apache crews. But for a considered view from a highly experienced and impartial observer one can cite Maj-Gen Edward M. Browne, the USA's Apache programme manager, who said:

"I think the Hellfire system is probably the most accurate and highly lethal anti-armor weapon that I have seen in the number of years I have been associated with anti-armor development". Like all good weapon systems, Hellfire is not standing still but exists in various growth versions and models with alternative guidance systems. Thanks to the modular design it is possible to change the seeker heads, three alternatives being IIR (imaging infrared), combined IIR and RF (radio frequency) or MM (very short millimetre-wave radar). Each has particular good and bad features, but a mix would give unrivalled capability in all battlefield conditions.

The Apache wings are designed to accept two launchers on each side. The launcher is of modular design and can be configured for either two or four rails. Loading Hellfires is easy, with automatic engagement with the rail and automatic latching and lock with the electrical connections guaranteed. The upper part of the launcher contains the missile control electronics, power supply and a safe/arm switch. An Apache prototype fired the first flight prototype Hellfire in March 1979, and production tests of the complete weapon system continued through to the end of January 1985. In numerous live firings the formidable 17lb (7.7kg) warhead has been shown to blast through any imaginable tank frontal armour, let alone thin roof plating, and this is partly because jet penetration depends upon the diameter of the shaped charge and the Hellfire head has a diameter of 7in (178mm). Today Hellfires are

Below: Reloading FFARs (2.75in-calibre folding-fin aircraft rockets) into a 19-tube launcher carried by a combat-ready Apache which already has a full load of Hellfires.

Above: The Hellfire laser-guided missile racked up an amazing record of accuracy during its development. In the Apache Test Program the accuracy record was 100 per cent, despite battlefield smoke obscuration, and lighting conditions ranging from brilliant sunshine to the blackest night engagements.

in full production, not only at Rockwell at a new plant outside Atlanta, Georgia, but also at Martin Marietta at Orlando, Florida.

In comparison, the rocket subsystem is relatively simple. The basic rocket has been a standard US munition for almost 35 years, but it has been subjected to ongoing development. It is a slim tube, originally known as 2.75in calibre but today officially known as 70mm. Most of its length is the solid rocket motor, originally the Mk 40 but in the latest rockets the new higher-thrust Mk 66 motor developed by the Navy. At the front is the interchangeable warhead, which is usually a straightforward HE type with variable fuzing. At the rear are the pivoted fins which, upon leaving the launcher tube, spring open automatically and spin the rocket to stabilize its flight.

Though a long-established weapon for use against both ground and aerial targets, it reaches a new peak of efficiency in the Apache. One advance is the option of an MSW (multipurpose submunition warhead) continuing numerous small but deadly bomblets. Another is articulating pylons. Rockets can be loaded on to all four pylons, and in this configuration each pylon can be automatically tilted according to the range input from the fire-control system; greater ranges resulting in exactly the right additional nose-up tilt. Another advance is the cockpit control subsystem. FFARs (folding-fin aircraft rockets) can be selected and fired by either crew-member, with aiming and steering commands shown on the IHADSS or in conjunction with the TADS for increased accuracy. The crew can select any desired fuze range or tree height to control detonation, as well as launching mode (singles, pairs or quads), launching rate, quantity launched and zone launching. Hughes Aircraft's Missile Systems Group at Canoga Park near Los Angeles, developed the LRLs (lightweight rocket launchers). By incorporating self-contained stores management, fuzing and fire control much weight has been saved. With four of the big M-261 launchers (19 tubes, or 76 rockets in all) the extra weight available for mission fuel is no less than 265lb (120kg). The smaller 7-tube launcher is the M-260. Minimum firing interval is 0.06 seconds in both launchers, and the whole system has single-switch BITE (built-in test equipment) after the rockets are loaded.

The 30mm gun

This leaves the only inbuild armament, the gun. It is remarkable how many modern attack helicopters today have no gun. In the view of the US Army a gun must be the primary AWS (area weapon subsystem), despite the considerable weight of the gun and, especially, the large quantity of ammunition. As noted earlier the Hughes solution was to design a new gun from scratch for this helicopter, and the

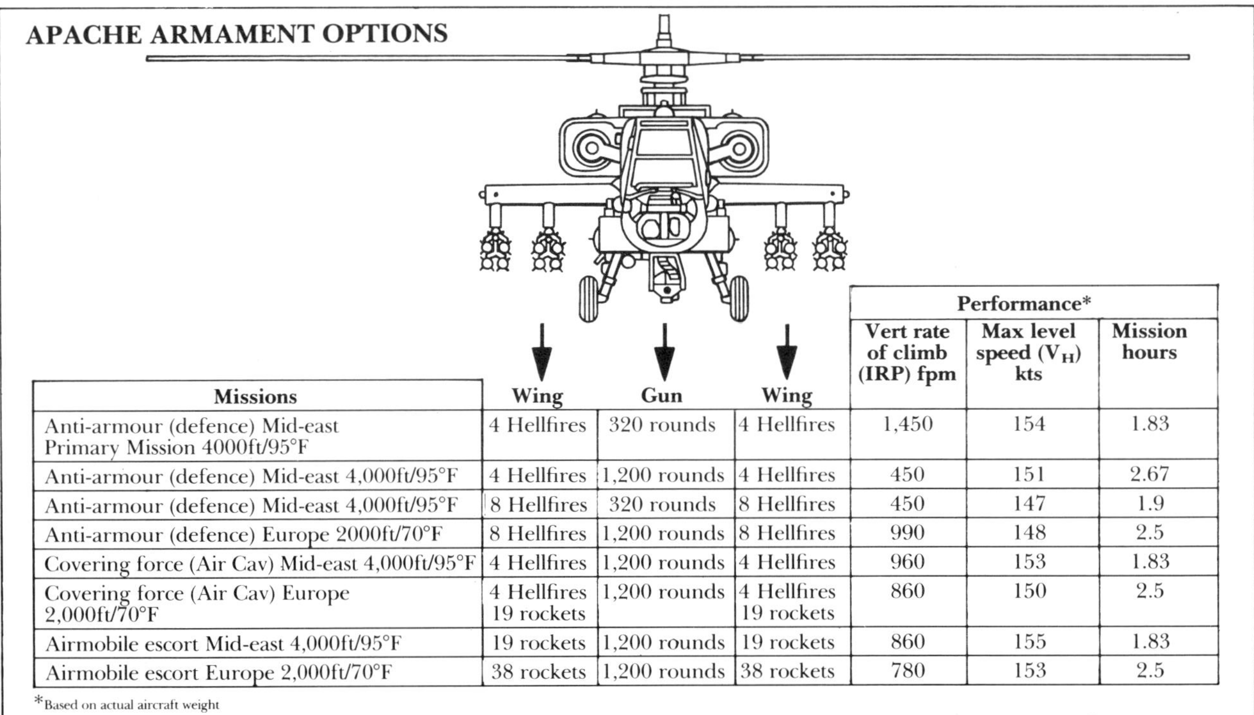

APACHE ARMAMENT OPTIONS

Missions	Wing	Gun	Wing	Performance*		
				Vert rate of climb (IRP) fpm	Max level speed (V_H) kts	Mission hours
Anti-armour (defence) Mid-east Primary Mission 4000ft/95°F	4 Hellfires	320 rounds	4 Hellfires	1,450	154	1.83
Anti-armour (defence) Mid-east 4,000ft/95°F	4 Hellfires	1,200 rounds	4 Hellfires	450	151	2.67
Anti-armour (defence) Mid-east 4,000ft/95°F	8 Hellfires	320 rounds	8 Hellfires	450	147	1.9
Anti-armour (defence) Europe 2000ft/70°F	8 Hellfires	1,200 rounds	8 Hellfires	990	148	2.5
Covering force (Air Cav) Mid-east 4,000ft/95°F	4 Hellfires	1,200 rounds	4 Hellfires	960	153	1.83
Covering force (Air Cav) Europe 2,000ft/70°F	4 Hellfires 19 rockets	1,200 rounds	4 Hellfires 19 rockets	860	150	2.5
Airmobile escort Mid-east 4,000ft/95°F	19 rockets	1,200 rounds	19 rockets	860	155	1.83
Airmobile escort Europe 2,000ft/70°F	38 rockets	1,200 rounds	38 rockets	780	153	2.5

*Based on actual aircraft weight

result could hardly have been more successful. The Hughes (now McDonnell Douglas) Ordnance Division at Culver City, Los Angeles, designed and now produces the gun, while Honeywell Defense Systems supplies the ammunition.

Chain Gun details

The gun is officially the M230, but it is commonly called the Chain Gun because of the way it works (today there are various smaller Chain Guns also). A powerful 30mm weapon, it has a single barrel and is externally powered by a 6.5hp motor. The unique feature when development began in December 1972 was the rotating bolt mechanism driven by an almost perfectly reliable chain. This permits a simplified gun cycle which has led to component lives and reliability certainly not exceeded, and seldom even approached, by any other automatic weapon. Long boltlock time ensures that virtually all gas escapes through the muzzle and not into the action, and the long dwell time ensures safety following a hangfire. The motor drive gives a powerful belt pull, eliminating the need for a powered ammunition booster, and there is no need for chargers, declutching feeders or other special devices. Further, as all the moving parts are totally keyed together, every motion is precisely controlled in magnitude and in timing. Equally important is the fact that, as each fresh round enters and passes through the gun, it is under absolute spatial and timing control at all times, eliminating virtually all normal ammunition feed problems.

New ammunition

The first XM230 prototype was fired in April 1973, with bursts fired the following month. In September of that year a 2,500-round Army trial was successfully completed. Two years later about 250,000 rounds of XM552 and XM639 ammunition had been fired through several Chain Guns with detail differences. In early 1976 the Department of Defense directed Hughes to rechamber the gun to fire Aden and DEFA ammunition to achieve NATO interoperability during Apache operations in Europe. Though manufactured now by Honeywell, this new ammunition was developed by Hughes, the three basic types of round being the M788 TP (target practice), M789 HEDP (high-explosive dual-purpose) and M799 HE (high-explosive). The modified gun, designated M230, was first fired in March 1978. The weight of the total gun system, without mounting, is 123lb (55.8kg); overall length is 64.5in (1,638mm). The gun can fire from single-shot up to 625 per minute.

Above: Fully armed Apaches are not normally rolled in service, especially near the rugged terrain of the US southwest. At least this view reveals many items along the underside.

Below: Apache stores: 16 Hellfire missiles and (L to R) fuel tanks, FFAR launchers, 30mm gun ammunition and, behind this, 2.75in FFAR rockets

In the Apache it is installed under the forward fuselage where, in a crash, it can safely be thrust up between the cockpits. The gun is completely exposed and hangs beneath a lightweight turret system normally locked in the central position with the gun held in the high-elevation position by springs. When selected, the gun is free to move according to the directions commanded by the IHADSS and TADS within azimuth limits of 100° to left or right and elevation limits of 11° up and 60° down. There are inviolable safety interlocks, the gun being controlled by a Lear Siegler electronic system. The basic gun can be supplied with either linked or linkless ammunition. In the Apache the ammunition is contained in a giant box in the bottom of the fuselage directly under the main rotor hub, with a capacity of 1,200 rounds. A linkless feed supplies the ammunition along the left side of the helicopter to the gun, a mirror-image duct on the right side returning the empty cases to the magazine.

Multipurpose weapon

The gun forms the primary area weapon, providing suppressive fire against main threat air defences and with the ability to destroy light armoured vehicles. It also has a considerable self-protection capability against air threats such as close-support aircraft and hostile helicopters, though of course not against a stand-off interceptor. The full ammunition load is normally carried except in exceptionally adverse circumstances such as 4,000ft (1,220m) altitude and a 95°F (35°C) environment when the standard loading is reduced to 320 rounds. Base Ten Systems supplies four avionic subsystems, two of which are the GCB and RC/MC. The former, the gun control box, controls gun firing, ammunition feed and dynamic braking of the gun drive motor. The rounds counter/magazine controller stores and updates the number of rounds remaining in the ammunition handling system. Base Ten's other two systems are the CPG's fire-control panel and its data-entry keyboard. Lear Siegler's TCB (turret control box) controls the actuators that aim the gun and compensate for its recoil. It electronically performs the complex filtering and control-law calculations necessary to put the gun exactly back on target after each shot has been fired. The TCB meets stringent accuracy requirements, re-aiming the gun ten times per second.

Below: The 30mm Chain Gun may be outperformed in some respects, but its reliability exceeds that of any other gun in its class. It is a product of McDonnell Douglas Helicopter Co. Reloading the magazine takes just 10 minutes.

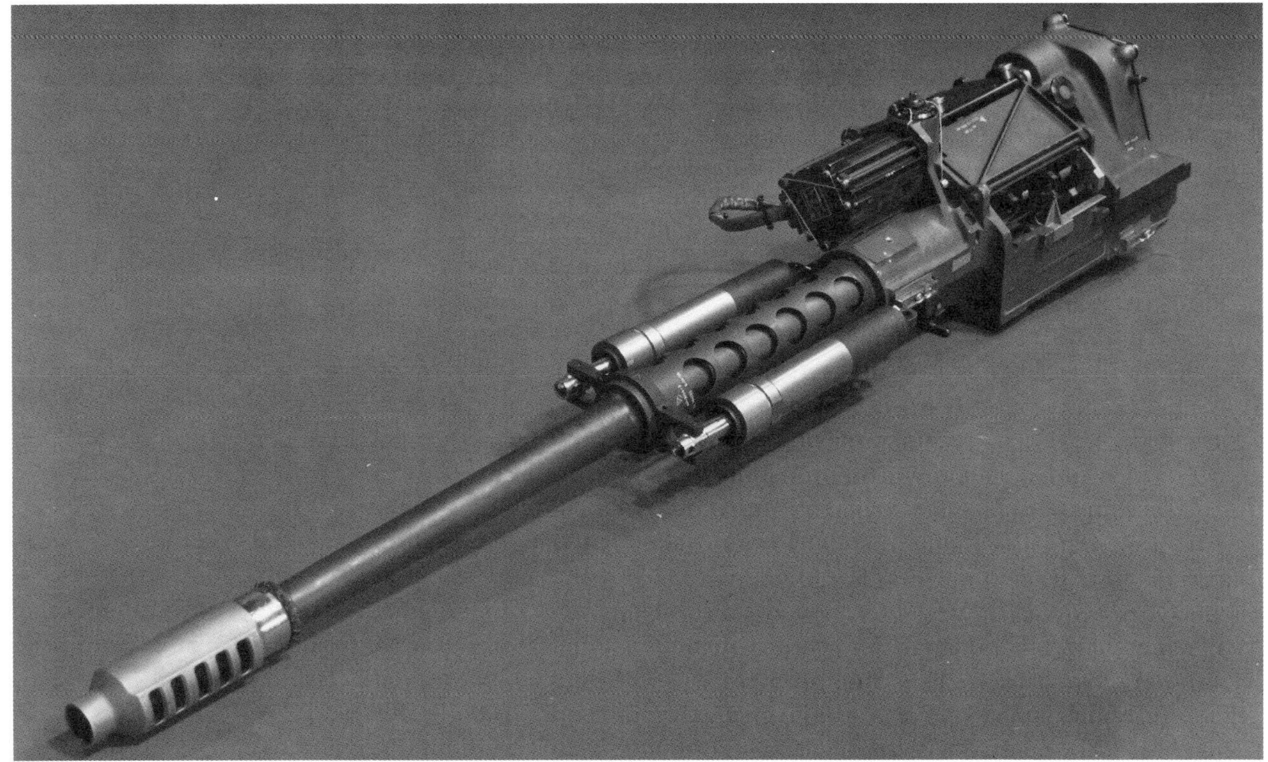

5

Joining the Army

DEVELOPING the AAH has taken very much longer than anyone anticipated 15 years ago, but the Army is getting a helicopter very much better than specification. For example, the primary mission demanded a VROC (vertical rate of climb) of 450ft/min while carrying eight Hellfires, 320 rounds of ammunition and fuel for 1.8 hours at the standard Army hot day of 4,000ft altitude and 95°F. Under these conditions the actual demonstrated VROC is no less than 1,450ft/min (7.4m/s), and Apaches have demonstrated sustained (not vertical) rates of climb exceeding 3,000ft/min (15.24m/s). It is this colossal sense of power and capability that so impresses every hard-bitten pilot who comes to the Apache.

The Army's enthusiasm

Top Brass are impressed too. The key man in the whole programme—and it is his job not to write advertising copy but to lean on the contractor—was the former AH-64 Program Manager, Maj-Gen Charles F. Drenz, USA. He has let his enthusiasm show many times in public, one comment being, "The Apache is a 24-hour machine, and we currently crew our ships on a 10-hour basis. I remember in Vietnam we used to fly our helicopters 8-10 hours a day, but we had to put them into maintenance all night long in order to get them up the next day. The Apache is different. The technology in this helicopter is similar to what we have in airliners today. These aircraft are continuously ready to take off with another load. It's the crews that must be changed. With the Apache's 24-hour availability, reliability, and the long service life we are going to get with this aircraft, we will need to double-crew this system—and this is good. . . . The Apache's extraordinary availability is further complemented by its speed and flexibility on the battlefield; it can move very quickly to wherever the ground commander wants it."

Assembly of the Apaches takes place in the totally new plant built at Mesa, Arizona, by Hughes Helicopters. On 6 January 1984 this company became a subsidiary of McDonnell Douglas, and on 27 August 1985 the name was changed to McDonnell Douglas Helicopter Company. But it was still Hughes when, on 30 September 1983, PV01, the Apache Production Vehicle 01, was ceremonially rolled out in the presence of many dignitaries and an Apache warrior on a white horse. At that time five other airframes had arrived from San Diego and were rapidly being turned into Apaches. Some idea of the work involved can be seen from the fact that, when the helicopters look finished, some 500 umbilical

Below: Apache air-loading procedures were certified at Sky Harbor Airport, Phoenix, on 22 June 1985 when Army and Air Force teams put six Apaches into this C-5A Galaxy.

connectors have to be checked along with 17,500 wire terminals and connectors. Each takes four days, using formidable computerized wire analysis systems. With just five Apaches on the line the Mesa facility looked empty, but it very quickly filled up and in 1986 reached its planned target of 12 helicopters a month.

At the rollout ceremony Jack Real, soon to retire as company president, promised that Hughes, and its Apache suppliers "in 36 states, Canada and West Germany [since joined by Israel Aircraft Industries, which produces the weapon pylon frame and rack] can be counted on to perform on the Army's No. 1 aviation program". Then the original first prototype YAH-64 whined into life and chief experimental test pilot Steve Hanvey put it through a breathtaking flight routine to show that it still worked, eight years to the day after its first flight.

21st Century machine

PV01 itself had to undergo prolonged checks before getting daylight under its wheels on 9 January 1984. Hanvey and copilot Ron Mosely were well pleased, and Jack Real made the comment: "The Apache must perform like a precision instrument and yet be extremely durable to live in the wild while serving the Army around the world well into the 21st Century."

Ahead of schedule, this machine was formally accepted by the Army on 26 January 1984. The Army nominated Hughes to win the Collier Trophy, the most coveted award in aerospace, and the National Aeronautic Association finally did pick the Apache as "the greatest achievement in aeronautics" for 1983. On 4 April 1984 the Army accepted PV02, and these first two production articles have ever since been instrumented and used in Arizona on Apache development. All subsequent helicopters have been delivered to the Army for training or combat duty in a massive programme which by 1990 aims to field 34 highly trained attack-helicopter battalions equipped with 612 Apaches in many parts of the world.

One of the largest yet most hidden facets of the programme was reported in a technical paper of 16 May 1984 on "software quality assurance". The Apache's numerous avionics boxes, sensors and weapon systems are provided by many suppliers, and are programmed in several computer languages. It may be possible in future aircraft to achieve a common language, but in the Apache it was Hughes' job to integrate all the contrasting systems to function harmoniously. Very complex and extensive test routines were devised for the software to prove that every system and weapon would work as a closely integrated whole. The result led not only to prolonged "debugging" of the software but also to physical engineering changes in the production helicopter.

In August 1984 PV02 scored two out of two with

Below: Apaches on crew training detail at Hanchey Army Heliport, near Fort Rucker, Alabama. This is one of the Training and Doctrine Command Schools.

the first production Hellfire missiles during tests at the Yuma Proving Ground. Subsequent tests included firings under varying conditions, rapid fire, ripples (salvos) and indirect fire with remote designation. In the same month SecDef Caspar Weinberger approved the final increment of 160 Apaches to bring the Army programme up to 675—160 more than the original plan. Unit flyaway cost in Fiscal Year 1984 dollars has been held close to $7.8 million, but this does not include such costs as support and training.

Apache training units

In 1984 training was all-important. The work began with the training of six instructors at Mesa and at Yuma. Initial key personnel training, completed in January 1985, used PV04-12 except for 08 and 10 which went to the Hunter-Liggett Reservation for operational testing with the OH-58D AHIP, which is tasked with designating Apache targets. The centre for Apache training is Fort Rucker, Alabama, backed up by Fort Gordon, Georgia, and Fort Eustis, Virginia. It moved on in September 1985 from the initial key course to the AQC (Aviator Qualification Course), joined by special courses for maintenance, avionics, weapons and other areas. The programme ran a little late, in that the first Apache delivered to TRADOC (Training and Doctrine Command) was not flown across the US to Fort Eustis until January 1985. Since then, 12 more have been delivered to Fort Eustis, to the ATALS (Army Transportation and Aviation Logistics School), where at Felker airfield 76 advanced training devices help qualify 900 maintenance test pilots and other personnel each year. In addition Fort Rucker and its satellite fields have received 32 Apaches and ten Cobras equipped with PNVS to handle the AQC.

Below: Head-on view of an Apache armed only with Hellfires at Echterdingen Army Airfield, near Stuttgart, Germany, near where the Apaches might one day be most needed.

On 4 April 1985 PV14 took off from Mesa at 7.30am local time, carrying four 230 US gal external tanks, and flown by two company pilots over Arizona and California, making a turn on the Pacific coast at Santa Barbara, and then landing back at Mesa at 3.30pm after covering 1,175 miles (1,891km). The 30min fuel reserve requirement was observed. At the same time the company announced that the Apache, in conformity with recent Defense Department mandates, was warranted (guaranteed) to meet or exceed stringent reliability requirements for two years or 240 flight hours. Any failure must be rectified with no cost to the United States government.

A little later, on 22 June 1985, six Apaches were loaded into a Military Airlift Command C-5A at Sky Harbor Airport, Phoenix, close to the Mesa plant. Air transport requires a certain amount of dismantling. The cavernous C-5 Galaxy airlifter is just able to swallow six of the big helicopters, twice the number that will go into the forthcoming C-17 and three times as many as fit inside the C-141B. In this first demonstration the Apaches were flown direct to waiting Fort Rucker.

Fielding the Apache

In October 1985 the massive task of "fielding"—getting the Apache into combat service—began in earnest with the start of instruction by the previously trained Army instructors. In the same month the Army accepted its 50th production Apache, most of them delivered in long cross-country flights. In December the 59th, last of the No. 2 production batch, was the first to go to Fort Hood, Texas, the giant single-station fielding location for all Apache combat unit training. Following completion of TRADOC individual training at Rucker, Eustis and (for avionics) Gordon, all Apache personnel go to Fort

Above: This Apache demonstrated self-deployment (from the USA to Europe, if necessary) by making flights of more than 1,100 miles (1,770km) with four 230 US gal external tanks.

Hood, join their combat unit and begin battalion-level training. This is administered by a special Apache Training Brigade, and a satellite Apache Program Office was established to manage all activity at Fort Hood, including Gray and Hood Army Airfields.

Today every Apache that comes off the Mesa line goes to Fort Hood. Here it is issued to one of the incoming battalions which, when it completes its long and intensive training programme, will fly its full complement of helicopters from Fort Hood to its own assigned home station, together with every item of support equipment needed to begin sustained combat operations. The first battalion was equipped at Fort Hood between February and April 1986, but this one, upon completion of its training cycle in 1987, is to remain at Fort Hood. Though fully combat-ready, its experience will be readily available to assist in the training programme.

Apaches in the reserves

In January 1986 two Apaches heading for Fort Eustis made a planned stopover at Raleigh-Durham Airport in North Carolina. Here they were surrounded by enthusiastic guardsmen from Company D, 28th Aviation Battalion, North Carolina Army National Guard. Back in January 1985 the NCARNG had been announced as the first guard or reserve unit to receive the Apache. Company D began sending aviators for the AQC course not long afterwards, and by late 1986 it expected to have 15 qualified pilots and 20 trained maintenance staff. It is to deploy with its 15 Apaches in late 1987, by which time several other guard units will have been named as recipients.

In April 1986 McDonnell Douglas Helicopters announced a new Vice-President in charge of the AH-64 programme: Stuart D. Dodge, who had previously had the corresponding job on the CH-47 Chinook at Boeing Vertol. Morton I. Leib was appointed Director, AH-64 Project Engineering, while William R. "Randy" McDonnell, son of the parent company's Board Chairman "Sandy" McDonnell, left the AV-8B Harrier II programme at St Louis to head the company's bid to win the LHX programme. LHX, the next-generation Army helicopter, includes an armed scout version but is in no sense a replacement for the Apache. The bigger helicopter is expected to continue for many years, and may well be the subject of further orders. In addition, of course, McDonnell Douglas Helicopter Company hope—with a great deal of confidence—to win export orders. Federal (West) Germany has been publicly named as a possibility for several years, despite its own halting participation in the PAH-2 part of the Eurocopter programme, and this explains that country's small share in the Apache production programme, AEG-Telefunken supplying the rotor-blade deicing control system. The later addition of Israel Aircraft Industries to the team also spotlights another potential customer, and a third country hardly likely to buy anything else is Japan.

Meanwhile, though no major change is expected to be introduced during manufacture of the 675 helicopters currently funded, McDonnell Douglas Helicopter has plenty of plans for improvements and upgrades. One is the prospect of new versions for the US Marine Corps and Navy, as outlined in the final chapter. Others concern the sensors, weapons and self-defence systems, the latter including increasing emphasis on low-observables "stealth" characteristics.

Another possibility is increasing use of composite structures. At present none of the primary structure, and only 4.1 per cent by weight of secondary structures, are of composites. But in October 1985 the company was awarded an $806,000 Army research contract to develop a new generation of composites for Apache secondary structure. These are expected to be fibre-reinforced thermosetting materials that are cheap to produce and fabricate, and resistant to high temperatures and to solvents. The new materials will be tested on the Apache nose-gearbox fairings which project from the centre of the engine inlets. According to MDHC composites chief Joy Sen, "If these materials prove effective, the research could be expanded to study the feasibility of using them for Apache primary structures such as the fuselage and rotor blades." This could have a significant beneficial effect on helicopter cost, and

Below: This Apache is actually in NOE (nap of the Earth) flight, almost touching the ground, during winter manoeuvres in early 1986 near Flagstaff, Arizona. Snow makes its presence obvious.

6
Marine and Navy Apaches

SEVERAL YEARS ago what was then Hughes Helicopters began studying what the very capable Apache might have to offer other US armed forces. It was difficult, certainly in the early 1980s, to establish a case for a US Air Force version, but in the case of the US Navy and Marine Corps the prospects looked much brighter. Neither service has anything with the combat capabilities of the Apache (though Sen Barry Goldwater has stated that the Apache costs less to buy than does the Marines' AH-1T Cobra, and has given figures to back up this contention—$9.8 million for the Cobra, and certainly the AH-1W SuperCobra will be much more expensive still). Be that as it may, and Goldwater is usually exceedingly well briefed, the Apache can do things that both seagoing US services would find very useful.

Even in its existing form the Apache can do a great all-year 24-hour job for the Marines. In 1983 Hughes appointed George Rock as manager of the company-initiated Marine Corps/Navy Apache Program, and in a low key began issuing public statements. In August 1984 a photograph was released showing a development Apache at the Mesa plant with Sidewinders on launch attachments—short cradles instead of the usual rail—on the tips of the helicopter's weapon wings. It was commented at the time that the Apache had been thoroughly proven in more than 8,000 hours of testing, and that the Marines could be offered deliveries as early as 1988. All the existing weapons and sensors would be retained.

Below: At the time of writing only one Apache, basically a regular AH-64A, had flown with Sidewinder AAMs. This particular Apache has since received further modifications, but McDonnell Douglas Helicopters has still not received any go-ahead on engineering development for the Marine version.

By 1985 McDonnell Douglas Helicopters had taken the concepts of Marine Corps and Navy variants much further. It had been agreed both would be powered by the same Dash-401 marinized version of the T700 engine as the SH-60B Seahawk helicopter. This would present virtually no problem, but the airframe and some equipment items would need additional protection against salt-water corrosion, drains wherever water might collect, upgraded wheel brakes, extra tiedown points, automatic powered folding of the main rotor (using a new hub design which permits two of the blades to pivot through 45° to be aligned with the fuselage) for storage in the hangers of surface vessels, doppler inertial navigation, enhanced EMR (electromagnetic radiation) shielding, and provisions for floating-base maintenance.

The proposed Marine Corps version was itself left little changed apart from major revision of its weapons. The 30mm Chain Gun was to be removed, because it would be likely to find limited use in air-to-ground operations and would "not be a suitable weapon for the air-to-air role". Likewise, though it appears to be a retrograde move to everyone except maker Hughes Aircraft, the Hellfires would be replaced by quadruple launchers for the TOW (probably TOW 2) wire-guided missile. TOW is already widely used by the Marine Corps, including the AH-1T Cobra helicopter. Other possible weapons which have been identified for this version include the massive 5in (127mm) Zuni attack rocket and the AIM-9L Sidewinder, the latter for air-to-air self-defence. There would be no change in the sensors carried.

For the Navy the prospects are more varied and the likely changes more extensive, though the latter would still hardly affect the basic helicopter, but only the mission equipment. The problem (or rather the challenge) is that there are several potential missions, including: CAP (combat air patrol) and escort, OTHT (over the horizon targeting), anti-shipping strike, and AEW (airborne early warning) surveillance in the absence of large aircraft carriers. By late 1985 the Navy helicopter was known as the Sea Apache, though it still (in mid-1986) remains a company initiative.

All versions would probably retain the TADS/PNVS sensors, though this is looking increasingly uncertain. A major addition, probably for all versions, would be a surface search and target-

Below: This artist's impression gives a clear early-1986 idea of what the proposed Navy Sea Apache would look like, in this case operating in the anti-ship role with four AGM-84 Harpoon cruise missiles. The exact arrangement of sensors, gun, and weapon has since been changed in detail, and may alter again.

acquisition radar, which could be mounted on a mast above the main rotor or, if the gun were to be removed, in a ventral installation. If the latter were chosen, the landing gears would probably be made to retract. In any case the tailwheel would need to be relocated further forward, because to meet Navy deck parking requirements the whole tail section would have to fold.

Sea Apache's weapons

In the OTHT and anti-shipping roles the Sea Apache would not need a gun, but could carry four AGM-84 Harpoon or AGM-119 Penguin cruise missiles. The company artwork shows a Sea Apache operating in this role with Harpoons, and also carrying the gun and Sidewinder AAMs. For CAP missions the radar would have to have good discrimination against aircraft far over the horizon. Operating from an escorting frigate or similar ship "on the fence" at the edge of the task force or battle group, the Sea Apache would take off armed with up to six AIM-9L or similar AAMs and either 1,200 rounds of 30mm ammunition or a correspondingly greater quantity of 20mm or 25mm ammunition, with the highest possible muzzle velocity. The helicopter would fly out along the bearing of the expected threat and then orbit at the speed for maximum endurance, either passively or actively monitoring the threat corridor. Threat aircraft can be autonomously detected, interrogated and engaged. This tactic is particularly effective during transits when the carrier is between launches, or at night, or when the carrier deck is locked (ie, not to be used). According to McDonnell Douglas Helicopter Company, the Sea Apache "offers the OTC (officer in tactical command) the flexibility to station a powerful strike capability out on the fence for day/night all-weather air defense".

A recent addition to the Sea Apache as at present envisaged is an automatic haul-down and deck locking system, if possible linked to powered traverse across the deck into or out of the hangar. This is seen as essential for rough-weather operations from frigate-class ships. Additional roles now being studied include escort and suppressive fire for SEAL (sea/air/land) operations, naval gunfire spotting and combat SAR (search and rescue) escort. Additional weapons being studied include Stinger close-range air-defence missiles, Sidearm anti-radar missiles derived from the Sidewinder, and various Service-specified cannon.

In September 1984 an Apache made a tour of facilities in the eastern US, in the course of which it called at: NAS Oceana, Norfolk, Virginia; USS *Intrepid,* the museum carrier parked on the Hudson River in New York City; and NAS Whiting Field, Milton, Florida. It spent almost a week at Oceana, and the visits certainly did nothing to harm the prospects for the proposed Navy and Marines versions.

AH-64A Specification **(Two-seat all-weather attack helicopter.)**

Engines. Two General Electric T700-GE-701 turboshafts. Power ratings: intermediate 1,694shp (1263kW) each; OEI contingency (one engine inoperative) 1,723shp (1285kW).
Dimensions. Diameter of rotors: main, 48ft 0in (14.63m); tail, 110in (2.79m). Length overall: tail rotor turning, 48ft 2in (14.63m); both rotors turning, 58ft 3.1in (17.76m). Height overall: over fin, 11ft 6.5in (3.52m); over tail rotor 14ft 0.6in (4.282m); over air-data sensor on main rotor, 15ft 2.9in (4.645m). Fuselage width at nacelles, 9ft 0.6in (2.758m). Tailplane (stabilator) span, 11ft 1.74in (3.397m). Wing span, 17ft 1.8in (5.227m). Track, 6ft 8in (2.03m). Wheelbase, 34ft 9in (10.59m). Main rotor disc area, 1,809.5sq ft (168.11m^2).

Weights. Empty (actual), 10,760lb (4,881kg). Internal fuel, 2,442lb (1,108kg). External stores (maximum except ferry mission), 1,700lb (771kg); (ferry, four tanks) 7,000lb (3,175kg). Gross weight (primary mission), 14,445lb (6,552kg); (maximum, ferry) 21,000lb (9,526kg).

Performance **(primary mission gross weight, intermediate rated power).**

	SL standard day	**4,000ft, 95°F**
Vertical rate of climb, ft (m)/min	2,460 (750)	1,450 (442)
Maximum rate of climb, ft (m)/min	3,200 (975)	2,570 (783)
Maximum level speed, kt (mph, km/h)	160 (184, 297)	155 (180, 289)
Cruise speed, max cont pwr, kt (mph, km/h)	160 (184, 297)	145 (169, 272)
Dive speed limit, kt (mph, km/h)	197 (227, 365)	197 (227, 365)
Max range internal fuel, nm (miles, km)	260 (299, 482)	280 (322, 519)
Endurance, internal fuel (h)	3.1	3.3
	Standard day	**95°F**
Hover in ground effect, ft (m)	15,000 (4,572)	10,200 (3,109)
Hover out of ground effect, ft (m)	11,500 (3,505)	7,000 (2,134)
Service ceiling, 2-eng, ft (m)	21,000 (6,400)	10,300 (3,139)
1-eng, ft (m)	10,800 (3,292)	6,400 (1,951)

PRINTED IN BELGIUM BY proost INTERNATIONAL BOOK PRODUCTION